M000046474

30-Day

Prayer
Challenge

for a

Less Stressed
Life

The

30-Day

Prayer
Challenge

for a

Less Stressed
Life

CAREY SCOTT

BARBOUR
PUBLISHING

© 2021 by Barbour Publishing, Inc.

ISBN 978-1-64352-832-8

All rights reserved. No part of this publication may be reproduced or transmitted for commercial purposes, except for brief quotations in printed reviews, without written permission of the publisher.

Churches and other noncommercial interests may reproduce portions of this book without the express written permission of Barbour Publishing, provided that the text does not exceed 500 words or 5 percent of the entire book, whichever is less, and that the text is not material quoted from another publisher. When reproducing text from this book, include the following credit line: "From *The 30-Day Prayer Challenge for a Less Stressed Life*, published by Barbour Publishing, Inc. Used by permission."

Scripture quotations marked TPT are from The Passion Translation®. Copyright © 2017, 2018 by Passion & Fire Ministries, Inc. Used by permission. All rights reserved. ThePassionTranslation.com.

Scripture quotations marked VOICE are from The Voice™. Copyright © 2008 by Ecclesia Bible Society. Used by permission. All rights reserved.

Scripture quotations marked AMPC are taken from the Amplified® Bible, Classic Edition © 1954, 1958, 1962, 1964, 1965, 1987 by The Lockman Foundation. Used by permission.

Scripture quotations marked AMP are taken from the Amplified® Bible, © 2015 by The Lockman Foundation. Used by permission.

Scripture quotations marked MSG are from *THE MESSAGE*. Copyright © by Eugene H. Peterson 1993, 1994, 1995, 1996, 2000, 2001, 2002. Used by permission of NavPress Publishing Group.

Published by Barbour Publishing, Inc., 1810 Barbour Drive, Uhrichsville, Ohio 44683, www.barbourbooks.com

Our mission is to inspire the world with the life-changing message of the Bible.

Printed in the United States of America.

WELCOME TO
THE 30-DAY PRAYER
CHALLENGE FOR A
LESS STRESSED LIFE!

Stress is something we will all face from time to time, but it doesn't have to take us out. The reality is that relationships will be hard, parenting will breed worry, finances will create concern, health will cause fear, and we will experience a million other anxiety-inducing moments in our lives. But when we invite the Lord into our stress and strife, we can find peace.

Let this book guide you into a new habit of seeking God's help as you navigate the frustrating parts of life. After a daily reading that will help you see things the way God does, there are questions to help you learn from your own thoughts and experiences. Do your best to be honest as you explore your answers, because it's the only way to really grow. Then, three prayers—morning, afternoon, and evening—will keep you thinking and praying about that topic all day so it will take root in your heart.

Friend, do the 30-day challenge for yourself. This gift of daily focus will not only cultivate a better understanding of how stress is affecting your life, but it will also create a deeper relationship with the One who promises to deliver you from it. And when you choose to walk out the truths you'll learn each day, you'll find perspective under pressure.

Day 1

THE RESTORATION OF "HAD" HOPE

"But three days ago the high priest and the rulers of the people sentenced him to death and had him crucified. We all hoped that he was the one who would redeem and rescue Israel."
LUKE 24:20-21 TPT

They *had* hoped, but now it was gone. These two disciples were walking on the road to Emmaus when a man—Jesus Himself—joined them. They didn't recognize Him and began to lament about their dashed hope in the Messiah. They *had* held on to expectations of Jesus being the One, but no more. Their faith *had* been strong as they put their confidence in Him, optimistic He would restore the nation of Israel, but when Jesus hung on that cross and died, so did their hope.

Can you imagine the letdown they must have felt? They'd been desperately waiting for a Savior, and the person they believed was an answer to their prayers appeared to be nothing more than a mere mortal. Their *hope* turned into *hoped*. It became past tense instead of active. Put yourself in their shoes for a moment and think about how they must have felt, especially after allowing themselves to grab on to the possibility.

The truth is that it's risky to hope at all because there's always a chance it will backfire. And when we decide to put our full confidence in someone or something, we hold on to hope with all we've got. It's present tense. We put all our eggs in one basket. But when a marriage falls apart or a child walks away in defiance, our dreams for the family we've always wanted crater. When the promotion we've been working toward falls through, our aspirations for the money to pay off debt go down in flames. A broken friendship rocks our foundation. And getting a scary diagnosis when we've lived health-consciously most of our life can bring into question the eating and exercise plans we've chosen to follow. These things create self-doubt. They cause us to question our wisdom and discernment. They move hope from current to expired. And in the end, hope is replaced by stress.

How do we keep anxiety at bay when life feels as if it's falling apart? How do we refuse to partner with worry when people or plans don't pan out? How do we keep hope in the present tense?

Choose to stay focused on the sovereignty of God. Choose to believe He will keep His promises—the ones in the Bible and the ones whispered into your heart. Decide God is continuing to work things out by closing doors and opening new ones. And activate your faith, holding on to it with white knuckles and all the grit you can muster.

The left turn in your life didn't catch God off guard. He is in every detail. He has your back. And when you take your *had* hopes to Him in prayer—surrendering your tears and fears—He will restore them to active hope again.

ASK YOURSELF THIS. . .

- *Where am I feeling hopeless in life right now?*

- *Whom do I talk to or what do I usually do in my own strength to work through the stress of bad hopes?*

- *Can I honestly say I've taken them to the Lord?*

- *What can I do today to restore my hope to active?*

PRAYER PROMPTS

Morning: Lay out your stress points to God and invite Him into your situation. Pray something like this: *Father, I am at the end of me. I feel hopeless and helpless. Would You please show me where You are in my situation? I need to see You.*

Afternoon: Tell God what your biggest areas of need are right now and that you are believing He will meet you there. Pray something like this: *Father, I'm struggling in these areas the very most and am activating my faith that You will restore my hope and joy. I know You are for me!*

Evening: Praise God for all He is doing right now that you may not be able to see. Pray something like this: *Father, You are the God of blessings and miracles. You're the One who can restore my "had" hope. I am expectant for Your hand in my life and grateful for all You will do!*

Day 2

THE KEY TO PEACE

---

*Pile your troubles on GOD's shoulders—he'll carry
your load, he'll help you out. He'll never
let good people topple into ruin.*
PSALM 55:22 MSG

For some reason, we've decided to put the weight of
the world on our shoulders. We not only worry about
all the things going wrong in our life, but we add to
that the cares of others. We're filled with anxiety about
our kids who are struggling in friendships and school-
work. We worry they don't feel good about themselves
as they navigate mean kids. We obsess over the fight
with our spouse, afraid they may throw their hands
in the air and walk away. Our heart grieves our aging
parents as we mourn the loss of who they were and are
heartbroken as we watch the effects of time or disease
overtake them, stressing about the details of their care.
We worry about our friends battling their own Goli-
aths. We're concerned for our country as we watch an
increase in hate and decline in morality. The financial
struggles of our church or our charity of choice keep
us up at night, searching for solutions to ease their
stress and strain. And the list goes on and on.

As women, we are innate caretakers. We have large storage tanks of compassion and empathy for the hurting. God created us to be relational creatures who need community. And we can multitask with the best of them. How wonderful that God made us this way! It seems only natural then that we would want to carry the emotional load for those we care about. Our heart for them is good, and we want to help however we can. The problem is that too often we do this in our own strength, and it leaves us overwhelmed and eventually ineffective.

Even more, rather than opening up and sharing our own troubles, we choose to keep them buried so we don't inconvenience or tax others. Including God. We rely on self to handle it all. We try to fix it. And it becomes too heavy to carry and we fall into the pit of despair and discouragement. That was never God's plan.

God is your partner as you love and care for yourself and others. You are His hands and feet, and He is your source and sustainer. It's in collaboration with Him that you can have the impact you desire. He is also your best emotional outlet because the Lord has broad shoulders to carry the hurts and heartaches that threaten to pull you under. And He invites you to pile your troubles—the ones you're facing or the ones you are helping others bear—on Him.

When you take them to God and ask for His intervention, you're recognizing that you are not the savior; He is. And that single act of surrender brings with it a beautiful gift of peace, settling in your spirit that you are not alone and help is on the way.

ASK YOURSELF THIS. . .

- *What are the big stressors I'm feeling today?*

- *Why do I put so much pressure on myself to hold everyone together and fix everyone's problems, including my own?*

- *Do I truly take my troubles to the Lord, expecting His help?*

- *What can I do right now that will lift my burdens and give me peace?*

PRAYER PROMPTS

Morning: List out your burdens to God and ask for His help. Pray something like this: *Father, I confess I haven't asked for Your help and have instead tried to handle it all myself. Thank You for caring about the things that trouble me. Here is what's worrying me right now. . . .*

Afternoon: Ask God to fill you with the peace of Jesus. Pray something like this: *Father, I'm struggling and stressed out and in desperate need of the peace only You can give. Would You exchange my worries for a stillness in my spirit? Would You quiet my fears? Would You bring harmony to my heartache?*

Evening: Thank God that He's willing to carry your burdens and always there to help. Pray something like this: *Father, my heart is full of gratitude for You. I'm humbled by Your unfailing and unwavering love for me. Thank You for being a safe place to share my troubles and a strong protector when I feel weak and overwhelmed. I love You!*

Day 3

BETTER TIME MANAGEMENT

*"Lord, help me to know how fleeting my time
on earth is. Help me to know how limited is
my life and that I'm only here but for a moment
more. What a brief time you've given me to live!
Compared to you my lifetime is nothing at all!
Nothing more than a puff of air. I'm gone so swiftly."*
PSALM 39:4-5 TPT

Have you ever said, "I need more time in the day!"?
Or maybe you've thought how life would be easier if
you had a personal assistant to help. We're so maxed
out that many of us would love to hire a nanny for our
kids and a cleaning service for our homes to free us
up to meet other demands. We utilize apps that
promise to help simplify our lives and read books that
promise to help us manage time like a boss. And even
with all of that, we still find ourselves enslaved to our
calendars, upside down with priorities, and bulging
with appointments and tasks every day. It feels like
there's simply too much to do and not enough hours
in the day to do it, and we're left feeling overwhelmed.
This kind of craziness keeps us from feeling in control and effective because we major on the minors
and minor on the majors. In the end, we're left with

a mountain of guilt and frustration that leaves us stressed out. We feel helpless and battle hopelessness that things can change.

The psalmist in today's verse asks a very interesting question. He wants the Lord to provide him with a divine reminder his life on earth is limited. Why do you think that is? It most certainly isn't because he wants more stress as he realizes he's running out of time. It's not to see what else he can pack into the day. Consider that he is asking because he's looking for perspective. He is hoping for focus so he can use his time and energy on what matters the most. Maybe he is looking for permission to not be everything to everyone so he can create margin for the right things.

What if you asked God for the same thing? Chances are, priorities are out of order somewhere. Maybe there are items on your to-do list that aren't vital, or vital things that need more of your attention. Maybe your calendar could use some decluttering and refocusing. Maybe you could work-block your day to help create better time management. Ask God to help you order your life so you're not frazzled and frenzied. Ask Him to show you where you need to focus your energy and effort. Friend, stress will melt away when you live and love following God's priorities for your life, trusting Him to give you everything you'll need to navigate your days with intentionality.

Grab hold of your time here on earth! Make the most of it! Choose to prioritize as you listen to God's leading. Learn to manage your time according to His plan. Don't skimp on those relationships or activities that top your list because they matter the most. And be the kind of woman who pursues living her best life and loving with gusto.

ASK YOURSELF THIS. . .

- *Honestly, how am I with managing my time?*

- *Do I see the connection between forgetting to prioritize my day and my stress level?*

- *What do I believe God is telling me about the value of time management?*

- *What needs to change so I can begin to take control of my day in positive ways?*

PRAYER PROMPTS

Morning: Confess the ways you've allowed life to overwhelm you. Pray something like this: *Father, I now see the connection between my crazy life and the stress I'm feeling. I'm sorry I've allowed these areas to get my time and attention over the ones I know are more important. I'm ready to make some changes.*

Afternoon: Ask God to speak into your heart His priorities for your life. Pray something like this: *Father, I want to know Your plans and hopes for my life here on earth. Please give me the spiritual ears to hear You. I am choosing to refocus my time in ways that honor You and benefit me. I'm listening.*

Evening: Praise the Lord for being alive and active in your life. Pray something like this: *Father, what a privilege to serve a God who cares so much about helping me organize my time so I can thrive. I'm thankful for Your willingness to teach me to prioritize and effectively reduce the stress I've been feeling. You're amazing!*

Day 4

THE OTHERS-FOCUSED
AGENDA

Don't let selfishness and prideful agendas
take over. Embrace true humility, and lift
your heads to extend love to others.
PHILIPPIANS 2:3 VOICE

When life feels out of control, women circle up the
wagons and give their full attention to manage the
chaos. We are so good at this! We're good at identi-
fying needs and making plans. We are protective and
ready to jump into action. God created us with a beautiful ability to sharply focus in on a broken marriage, a
troubled child, a dwindling bank account, or a health
hurdle. We aren't afraid to get our hands dirty. We
fight for what we love, and we're reliable in a pinch.
But our natural reflex is to become selfish, expending
all our energy on ourselves and the messiness of our
life. What gets us into trouble is when we forget to
look up at the Lord and out at the community He's
given us.

Of course, it's prudent to be present in our circumstances. There are some seasons that kick us in the

backside and we're just trying to keep our head above water. Without question, life requires our attention and action on so many levels. But sometimes the best thing for our own anxious heart is to reach out to friends and family and check on theirs. It's vital to look up and out, to connect with those around us in meaningful ways, to talk about something other than our mess. Doing so offers us a mental break, allowing us to see the needs of others. It affords us the space necessary to see the hurts and heartaches those around us are facing. It brings perspective. And it frees us up to love and support those who need it.

Jesus was so good at this. There were times in His ministry when He chose to remove Himself from the masses, and even the disciples, to regroup, refocus, and reconnect with the Father in prayer. Jesus knew the value of solitude to work through what lay ahead for Him. He was self-aware and took care of His needs, knowing when to create space to deal with personal struggles and challenges. But He didn't stay there. Jesus didn't stay exclusively self-focused, especially not at the risk of others. His agenda—above all else—was to love the world. And it's this example that provides us with a powerful motivation for how we should live our own lives.

It does a heart good to serve others; we are compassionate and empathetic creatures. And the amazing thing is that doing so brings with it an unexpected blessing of fulfillment. We feel better about our own life when we pour into someone else's. It allows us to gain perspective and depth. And while we may choose to create an agenda that helps us love on others, God in His generosity loves on us.

ASK YOURSELF THIS. . .

- *Is my agenda right now selfish or selfless?*

- *Do I see a connection between stress and self-focus, peace and being others-focused?*

- *Whom do I need to reach out to today to offer support and love?*

- *What needs to change so my agenda is balanced according to God's plan?*

PRAYER PROMPTS

Morning: Talk to God about the kind of agenda—knowingly or unknowingly—that you've been following. Pray something like this: *Father, thank You for opening my eyes to how I've been living my life. I'm aware of it now and will be making the right adjustments to make sure I find the balance between self-care and being others-focused.*

Afternoon: Understanding its value and importance, ask God to help you look up at Him and out at your community. Pray something like this: *Father, I recognize the benefits of looking up and out instead of putting all the focus on me and my struggles. I'm going to need Your gentle reminder to focus on others in those times I am overwhelmed with my own stuff. Train me to have perspective.*

Evening: Thank God for the unexpected blessings that come with being others-focused. Pray something like this: *Father, I love how You've made it possible for me to be blessed in those times I choose to bless those around me with my compassion and empathy. I'm amazed at how You have thought of everything. Thank You!*

Day 5

YOU HAVE A HOLY ADVOCATE

*Meanwhile, the moment we get tired in the waiting,
God's Spirit is right alongside helping us along. If we
don't know how or what to pray, it doesn't matter. He
does our praying in and for us, making prayer out of
our wordless sighs, our aching groans. He knows us far
better than we know ourselves, knows our pregnant
condition, and keeps us present before God. That's
why we can be so sure that every detail in our lives
of love for God is worked into something good.*
ROMANS 8:26-28 MSG

We may be caught off guard by unforeseen circumstances colliding into our lives, but God never is.
When life throws a curveball, our surprised reaction
doesn't mirror the Lord's because He knew it was
coming. Even more, He allowed it. And only because
in the end, God knew it would be for our benefit and
His glory. It would be for the greater good in our life.

But here's the gold nugget shined up just for you.
Don't miss the part in today's scripture where it says
the Holy Spirit is with you in those stressful times.
His job is to help as you walk out the day to day. It's
not only His strength and courage that's available to

you. The Spirit will give you more than wisdom and discernment. While He is empowering you with confidence and comforting you with the peace of Jesus, the Holy Spirit is also doing something downright amazing. He prays for you.

Can you remember a time you were so afraid that you couldn't find the words to pray? Or a time when your heart was so broken, your prayers were nothing more than tantrums and tears? Maybe there was a moment of shock and your mind couldn't come up with the right words to ask for God's help. Chances are you've been in that exact situation more than once. Haven't we all?

How wonderful then to realize that the Holy Spirit—who knows you better than you could ever know yourself—talks to the Father for you. On your behalf, He explains the deepest details of the stress and anxiety you're facing. Maybe all you can do is grunt or groan in emotional pain. Maybe silent weeping is all you can muster. Maybe, like many, you sit stunned and unable to form a sentence to describe what you are feeling or what you need. Regardless of whether you can speak eloquently or not at all, the Holy Spirit knows exactly what's going on in your heart. He understands the complexity of your emotions. And He promises to share them with God in great detail.

Find peace in knowing the Lord is fully aware of the stress you're feeling, and find hope knowing He's aware of what you need to calm your anxious heart.

ASK YOURSELF THIS. . .

- *What is my stress level right now, and why?*

- *What is my understanding of how the Holy Spirit works in my life?*

- *How do I feel knowing the Holy Spirit prays for me? What is my response?*

- *How does this knowledge affect my anxious heart?*

PRAYER PROMPTS

Morning: Ask God to show you where He is in your difficult situation. Pray something like this: *Father, I'm glad to know You allow things only for my benefit and Your glory, but I'm struggling to see Your hand in my life right now. Will You show me where You are and offer me divine perspective?*

Afternoon: Confess your misunderstandings about the Holy Spirit's role in your life. Pray something like this: *Father, I haven't understood the gift of the Holy Spirit. Instead of acknowledging and embracing Him, I've ignored Him. Help me remember the Spirit is my advocate on every level. What a blessing!*

Evening: Thank God that He has full and complete understanding of your anxious heart, even when you don't. Pray something like this: *Father, I'm so grateful that You know me fully. What a relief to realize I don't have to find the words to share how I feel because You already know. Even more, You're already in action to help me find peace and comfort.*

Day 6

THE BENEFIT OF WISDOM
AND DISCERNMENT

My child, never drift off course from these two goals
for your life: to walk in wisdom and to discover
discernment. Don't ever forget how they empower
you. For they strengthen you inside and out and
inspire you to do what's right; you will be energized
and refreshed by the healing they bring. They give
you living hope to guide you, and not one of life's tests
will cause you to stumble. You will sleep like a baby,
safe and sound—your rest will be sweet and secure.
PROVERBS 3:21-24 TPT

According to the writer, the pursuit of wisdom and discernment should be intentional goals for living because they have the unique ability to empower you. A well-thought-out plan curbs anxiety because you've put in the effort to look at all the angles. You've taken the time to consider unforeseen possibilities. You've sought insight from trusted mentors and asked God to help you. Maybe you've researched all the options and studied how others have handled certain situations. All of these things are good! When you are deliberate in decision-making, it helps manage the stress when things don't go as planned.

Even more, seeking God's wisdom has a special way of building a steadfast strength in you that's unmatched. It creates confidence and courage, inspiring you to stand up and make the right choices. Being wise and discerning is key to feeling energized as you take the next right step, which is often also a challenging one. And involving the Lord in your desire for smart living provides you with hope for the future, alleviating worry. It guides you to desire good and righteous options that trump tension and trauma.

Stress is an epidemic in today's world. If you think about it, stress thrives when we are playing catch-up to bad decisions. When we're trying to undo what a thoughtless choice tangled, it causes us to burn with anxiety. When we move in a direction that we know isn't sane or sensible, panic begins to rise. We lose our joy and struggle to find peace. Sleep eludes us because we're apprehensive about the consequences that may follow a hasty move. It's just a horrible feeling all the way around.

Can you remember a time when you tossed wisdom out the window because you felt rushed to make a decision? Or can you honestly admit this is how you're living right now? Are you frantically making choices that really need more time to marinate? Have you grown tired of waiting for God to answer, so you've decided to move forward with your own heart's desire? Choose today to take a step back and evaluate your motives and outcomes. Be bold enough to take a time-out to seek wisdom and discernment. Trust God to show you His plan for your life. And know that when you do, scripture says you'll sleep safe and sound. Just like a baby, your rest will be sweet and secure. . .and stress-free.

ASK YOURSELF THIS. . .

- *Am I a seeker of wisdom?*

- *Do I make choices in haste, or do I take my time to think through them?*

- *What correlation do I see between my bad choices and my stress level?*

- *How does God fit into my decision-making?*

PRAYER PROMPTS

Morning: Ask God to help you make wisdom and discernment goals for your life. Pray something like this: *Father, I need Your help to see the value of living smart. Would You please give me reminders to seek You in all my decisions, so I don't make rash judgment calls that set me up for anxiety?*

Afternoon: Confess the times you've purposefully left God out of the decision-making process because you were in a hurry or didn't like His leading. Pray something like this: *Father, thank You for grace. Thank You for Jesus' gift of the cross. Thank You that there's nothing I can do to remove Your love from me. I'm sorry for the times I've left You out of my decisions; I don't want to do that anymore.*

Evening: Invite God into all decisions from this point forward. Let Him know you trust Him and need His wisdom. Pray something like this: *Father, I trust that You know what's best for me. I believe You will show me wisdom in my next steps if I seek You. I have faith You will give me a discerning spirit fueled by Your Holy Spirit. I will wait for Your plan to unfold and follow it.*

Day 7

GO RIGHT TO GOD

*Come to Me, all who are weary and burdened,
and I will give you rest. Put My yoke upon your
shoulders—it might appear heavy at first, but it
is perfectly fitted to your curves. Learn from Me,
for I am gentle and humble of heart. When you
are yoked to Me, your weary souls will find rest.
For My yoke is easy, and My burden is light.*
MATTHEW 11:28–30 VOICE

Where do you go when you're burdened with the
storms of life? Maybe you go to Netflix, looking for
a series to binge-watch to escape the chaos. Maybe
you grab a favorite beverage or a tub of your favorite
ice cream or a good book. Maybe you go for a quick
run or you blare your favorite music and sing along.
Whom do you reach out to, anxious to ruminate over
the situation at hand? Maybe it's your mom, a close
friend, your spouse, a small-group leader, a coworker,
or someone from a support group. What would you
add to the list? The truth is that we all have our go-tos
when circumstances feel stressful and suffocating. We
want to feel better. We need to find relief. And in our
resilience, we're desperate and determined to find a

way to manage our anxieties and insecurities. . .one way or another.

But, friend, when the worries of life seem overwhelming, do you take them to the Lord? Today's passage offers a power-packed reminder of the benefits that come from going right to God. Look back and find the one word that sums up the divine exchange that takes place. When you go right to God with a heavy heart full of fear and frustrations, He gives you *rest*. Ice cream may be yummy, but it can't do that.

The problem is that stress has a special way of stirring up our stress levels, keeping us focused on not only the crazy we're dealing with right now but also the inevitability of horrible outcomes and endings heading our way. At least that's what we think is right around the corner. Too often, we forecast doom and gloom. Amen? And rather than take God up on His offer to off-load our anxiety on Him, we become frantic and our coping skills go into overdrive. We decide we can (and will) fix it ourselves. And we work toward man-made solutions that may offer temporary solutions at best but no long-term relief. In the end, we're right back where we started and more stressed out than ever.

Take a deep breath, friend. Why not try it God's way? Take time today and talk to Him about what's bothering you. Lay out all your fears and insecurities. Tell the

Lord about the ways you're feeling shaken and unsure about life. Cry those tears—the ugly ones—and pour out your heart to the only One who can bring lasting peace. The plan was never for you to figure it out all by yourself! Instead, the plan has always been for Him to carry the stress-inducing heavy burdens for you. Go ahead and give it a whirl. You have nothing to lose and a whole lot of emotional rest to gain.

ASK YOURSELF THIS. . .

- *Where do I go when life gets stressful?*

- *Who was it that made me think I needed to handle everything on my own?*

- *Do I honestly believe God will carry burdens for me?*

- *What do I need to change so I can walk in the truth of this passage of scripture?*

PRAYER PROMPTS

Morning: Lay out your burdens—big and small—to God, and then ask Him to take them from you. Pray something like this: *Father, I'm struggling and stressed out by these things right now. I feel overwhelmed and underwater. My heart feels hopeless. And honestly, I am scared that things will never change and that I'm messing up everything. Please take these from me. I need Your help right now.*

Afternoon: Tell God about the ways you've coped with difficulties in the past, thinking you could fix everything. Pray something like this: *Father, sometimes I think I can handle everything on my own. I know I've been that way most of my life, and I'm asking for forgiveness for not trusting You. I recognize You are God and I am not. I'm going to put my faith in You fully from this point forward.*

Evening: Praise the Lord for His willingness to carry your burden and exchange it for rest. Pray something like this: *Father, only You can offer something so beautiful. I'm full of gratitude because You love me so much that You're willing to take the stresses of today off my shoulders and replace them with emotional, mental, and physical rest. No one else can do that! You are absolutely amazing, and I love You!*

Day 8

THE STRESS OF
BUSY THOUGHTS

---

*Whenever my busy thoughts were out of control,
the soothing comfort of your presence calmed
me down and overwhelmed me with delight.*
PSALM 94:19 TPT

Sometimes it feels like our lives are way too busy. We're overworked, overscheduled, and overwhelmed. From food prep to car pool to career to volunteer hours to bedtime routines, we toil and labor at our seemingly endless to-do list from the moment we open our eyes in the morning until our head hits the pillow in exhaustion at night. On the regular, we wear ourselves out and cannot wait for sleep. But once we crawl into bed with expectations of sweet slumber, the battle with those pesky busy thoughts begins.

Friend, what is it that keeps you up at night? What worries wake you at two in the morning? What are the concerns that rob you of sleep?

Maybe you are scared about your finances because the money needed for bills is more than the money in your checking account. Maybe your friend received a diagnosis that is sure to be an uphill battle, and you don't want to lose her. Maybe you're not sure how to help your aging parent and are struggling to find a clear answer. Are you worried about your job? Are you obsessing over what someone said to you in anger? Do you stress about never finding someone to marry or never having kids? Or maybe you have anxiety over the marriage you're in and the kids you have, feeling like both are headed in the wrong direction. Certainly there is no shortage of stress-inducing situations and circumstances. That's for sure.

Even the psalmist had thoughts that got away from him. He had fears and insecurities play on repeat in his mind. It's a common battle that connects us as humans. And God—in His graciousness—knew this would be an ongoing issue and made a way to calm our anxious hearts. Notice how the writer understood the power of the Lord's presence. He knew that inviting God into his madness not only calmed him down but also brought deep delight. It's a powerful exchange if you think about it. He promises to comfort you in unmatched ways when you ask for His help.

When the busy thoughts refuse to leave you alone and instead keep you up at night, you have a decision to make. You can allow your mind to ruminate on them over and over and over again, picking apart the details and playing out scenarios full of horrible outcomes and endings. Or you can choose to give them all to God, asking Him to bring peace and a sense of calm into the stress. You can think back on all the times He came through and all the ways He straightened out your crooked path. You can speak out scripture reminders that God is in control and is always with you. And when you choose to involve the Lord in your middle-of-the-night busy thoughts, you will find rest.

ASK YOURSELF THIS. . .

- *What are the busy thoughts that are keeping me up at night?*

- *In what ways have I tried to fix my sleepless nights, and have any of them worked?*

- *Have I ever asked the Lord to calm my anxious heart?*

- *What do I feel the Holy Spirit is speaking to me right now?*

PRAYER PROMPTS

Morning: Talk to the Lord about the fears and insecurities you're battling at night. Pray something like this: *Father, there are things I'm struggling with that are robbing me of peace and sleep. I am afraid, always focusing on possible outcomes and endings that are horrible. I am worried about things I cannot fix. I need Your help.*

Afternoon: Ask God to give you the eyes and ears so you can understand His perspective on the stressors in your life. Pray something like this: *Father, would You speak into my heart and tell me Your thoughts on the things keeping me awake at night? I need to hear Your perspective because I know it will bring me peace and rest.*

Evening: Thank the Lord for how He has showed up in your life before. Recount from memory times He made a way or calmed a storm. Pray something like this: *Father, I remember situations where You intervened and made right something very wrong. I remember circumstances where You brought understanding and healing. Thank You for always showing up for me. My heart is full as I recount Your goodness.*

Day 9

INSTEAD

Don't fret or worry. Instead of worrying, pray.
Let petitions and praises shape your worries into
prayers, letting God know your concerns. Before
you know it, a sense of God's wholeness, everything
coming together for good, will come and settle
you down. It's wonderful what happens when Christ
displaces worry at the center of your life.
PHILIPPIANS 4:6–7 MSG

Let's just be honest, there is so much to worry about
these days, isn't there? And while we know we shouldn't
lose our mind and instead trust God. . .it's hard. It's
hard to trust someone you cannot see or touch. What
we want is for someone to hold our hand, affirm us,
and remind us everything will be okay. We want a
friend who will sit across from us at coffee and tell
us how to fix our fears. We want someone to offer to
handle it for us because our worry is exhausting and
has woken up every insecurity known to mankind. We
want to be engulfed in a reassuring bear hug. We may
even want to walk away and start over. And for many,
we're just one more concern away from a complete
breakdown. Friend, you are not alone.

Life is big and scary, and it's full of uncertainty. There is no way around that reality. It's a truth we'll face until we meet Jesus face-to-face. On the regular, we can expect our foundation to be rocked, circumstances to change unexpectedly, and life to throw us plenty of curveballs. And while these things can set off alarm bells in our heart and breed all kinds of anxiety, what if we decided to handle them differently next time?

Today's verse offers a challenge, and it's a biggie. The writer, Paul, is encouraging us to consider another option—another perspective when life gut punches us. Reread the first two sentences of today's scripture passage out loud, putting your name at the beginning. The challenge is designed to change your reaction when the bad news hits. When you're discouraged, Paul is daring you to respond differently. Before you call Aunt June or your bestie in tears, before you buy junk food and numb out on Netflix, before you work yourself into a tizzy and your blood pressure level goes through the roof. . .pray. Because when you decide to immediately take your worries and anxieties to God, you will sense the Lord's presence in profound ways. It may not always be the easy thing to do, but it will be the most beneficial. And because of your faith-filled response, He will bring peace to calm your anxious heart.

Freaking out may have been your default button to discouragement. Your first response to anxiety may have been to melt down into a messy puddle of inconsolable tears. But because you are a woman full of faith, choose today to change things up. Not only will taking everything to prayer first benefit you; it will also teach those around you to respond the same. Life may never be calm, but with God's help, you can be.

ASK YOURSELF THIS. . .

- *What is usually my first response to stress and worry?*

- *Can I honestly say I've gone to God with my concerns?*

- *Do I really believe the Lord can help me in this way?*

- *How will I remember to stop and pray when anxiety hits next time rather than go to my usual places of comfort?*

PRAYER PROMPTS

Morning: Confess to the Lord all the people, places, and processes you used to calm your anxiety in the past. Pray something like this: *Father, forgive me for putting people, places, and processes above You. For so long, I've chosen to trust others for comfort. I know You are the One who can bring the peace I need when life throws a curveball, and to You I will go. Thank You for caring about the details of my life.*

Afternoon: Share with God what is heavy on your heart today and tell Him what you need. Pray something like this: *Father, I am so stressed out and worried about these things. I'm asking for Your help to calm me down and give me Your peace. My faith tells me I can trust an unknown outcome to a known God, and I am choosing to cling to that today.*

Evening: Ask God to help make Him your default button when things feel overwhelming and stressful. Pray something like this: *Father, I want You to be the first place I go for peace and comfort. I want You to be top-of-mind during troubled times. Let Your Holy Spirit be quick to prompt me to lay my burdens at Your feet. There is no substitute for Your presence.*

Day 10

YOU ARE LOVED. . .
NO MATTER WHAT

Can anyone be so bold as to level a charge against
God's chosen? Especially since God's "not guilty"
verdict is already declared. Who has the authority
to condemn? Jesus the Anointed who died, but more
importantly, conquered death when He was raised to
sit at the right hand of God where He pleads on
our behalf. So who can separate us? What can come
between us and the love of God's Anointed? Can
troubles, hardships, persecution, hunger, poverty, danger,
or even death? The answer is, absolutely nothing.
ROMANS 8:33–35 VOICE

There are few things that can put a pit in your stomach more than being accused of wrongdoing. Be it true or not, when you're condemned by someone you thought had your back, it feels like betrayal on epic levels. And even if your motives were pure and it was a complete misunderstanding, sometimes the damage is done. Maybe it was a lapse in judgment and you never meant to inflict pain, but the finger was pointed anyway. Your peace is gone, replaced with guilt and shame. And as you replay the situation over and over and over again in your mind, worry and anxiety take over.

The truth is that we all mess up and heartfelt apologies are often needed. Hard conversations are usually necessary. And chances are it may take time to rebuild trust and gain back the ground that was lost. But that doesn't mean you're required to sit in the seat of condemnation, feeling worthless and unlovable.

It's important to remember that you are God's chosen, and His Son, Jesus, died on the cross for every sin you have or ever will commit. You are not perfect—not by a mile—nor are you expected to be. Misjudgments, miscalculations, and mishaps are part of the human experience, something we all have in common. And while there can be painful consequences attached to your choices, you're not required to stay in the proverbial doghouse forever. You don't have to take verbal abuse or be a human punching bag for others. And you don't have to remain tangled in stress, beating yourself up for making a mistake. Take a deep breath, friend.

The Word of God is clear when it says there's nothing you can ever do—no bad decision, no mistake, no malicious intent, no error in judgment—that will change how God feels about you. Honestly, you're not powerful enough or capable of doing anything to compromise His love for you. That is good news!

So, when others level charges against you, this is the promise you cling to. When someone is trying to make you feel small for messing up, reread these verses. When they decide to hold on to bitterness and anger, it's not the end of the world. And when the burden feels so heavy that you're drowning in stress, ask God to remind you of His unfailing love.

Others may refuse to extend grace and try to make you "pay" for it, but remember Jesus already did. And because of that, you are fully loved and completely forgiven. And nothing can undo what's been done.

ASK YOURSELF THIS. . .

- *Who are my accusers right now?*

- *How has their response to my intentional or accidental wrongdoing affected me?*

- *Do I honestly believe God loves me no matter what and paid the price for my sins?*

- *Once I've repented, how can I keep from sitting in self-condemnation, beating myself up with guilt and shame?*

PRAYER PROMPTS

Morning: Pour out your heart, telling the Lord the situations where you feel condemned and unloved. Pray something like this: *Father, I feel so overwhelmed right now. I am being beat up for messing up, and I feel so alone.*

Afternoon: Pray for your accusers. Ask God to bless them and prosper them. Pray something like this: *Father, I know You tell us to pray for our enemies, and I don't do that very often. Hear my prayers for them today, and bless them in new and fresh ways. Let them feel Your presence in their lives. Show them they are loved.*

Evening: Ask God to lead you in letting go and moving forward after you've fully repented. Pray something like this: *Lord, I ask that Your mercy and forgiveness wash over me. I am sorry to You and to those I have let down. Do not allow me to wallow in my shame. I know that each time I repent, I am made whole in Your unfailing love.*

Day 11

PEACE TO REPLACE
THE STRESS

---

*Blessed [happy, spiritually prosperous, favored by God]
is the man who is steadfast under trial and perseveres
when tempted; for when he has passed the test and
been approved, he will receive the [victor's] crown of
life which the Lord has promised to those who love Him.*
JAMES 1:12 AMP

Let's just be honest here. It is stinkin' hard to be unwavering in our faith when we're facing spine-weakening and joy-draining trials in life. When it all hits the fan, holding on to the belief that we'll get to the other side of the chaos intact is often a tall order. It feels impossible and we want to give up. We lose hope. We consider waving the proverbial white flag and limping away to lick our wounds. Rather than cling to the Lord, we give in to the fear of possible horrible outcomes and endings. Instead of believing God is fully engaged in our situation, we grab control and try to fix things ourselves. We aren't steadfast or full of perseverance, and we end up stressed out, overwhelmed, and scared.

Some people may offer encouragement, saying God will never give you more than you can handle. It's a common response full of good intentions, but it's not solid theology. The truth is that He will absolutely give you more than you can handle on your own—more than every bit of your human strength can withstand—because God never intended for you to deal with this crazy and unpredictable life without Him. Going it alone wasn't part of His plan. From the beginning, God promised to be with you always. And if we take Him up on His offer, the Lord's presence will offer peace to replace the stress.

Take a personal inventory. Think about the places where you are feeling pressed on all sides. Maybe your marriage seems to be spiraling out of control or you feel helpless to support your child dealing with bullies at school. Maybe you think time is ticking away and you'll never find a spouse or be able to get pregnant and have children. It could be concern about your finances and being able to pay the bills stacking up. Maybe there are rumors of layoffs or pay cuts at work. Life is hard, and there will always be something trying to steal your joy. There will always be some fear that looks bigger than your faith can handle. And there will always be plenty of situations that stress you out and make you want to walk away in defeat. How are you responding?

We are all limited by our human condition, pure and simple. You may be very wise, have epic integrity, and have a strong moral compass. . .but it's not enough to navigate trials and temptations you'll face. You may have a great support system in place, but that team can't do what only God can.

And even more, there's a beautiful blessing that comes from choosing to remain steadfast and persevere when life takes a hard left turn. Today's verse reminds us that if we do, we will be fun, faith-filled, and favored. So, friend, take your stresses to the Lord and trust that He will give you all you need to make it through. You are so loved.

ASK YOURSELF THIS. . .

- *Am I trusting the Lord with my fears right now?*

- *Where am I trying to fix things myself?*

- *Why do I struggle to believe God can and will help me manage my stress level?*

- *What do I need to change so I can be blessed for my steadfastness and perseverance?*

PRAYER PROMPTS

Morning: Confess the times your faith hasn't been strong enough to trust God over your own efforts. Pray something like this: *Father, sometimes I think I can handle things better than You. I confess my lack of faith and admit my need for Your intervention in my life.*

Afternoon: Tell the Lord where you're feeling stressed and afraid. Surrender your control and ask for His help. Pray something like this: *Father, I'm worried about these things right now. I keep imagining horrible outcomes and endings and it's scaring me. I am laying them at Your feet, asking for Your help as I navigate my way through them. Please give me peace.*

Evening: Thank God for blessings that come from obedience. Pray something like this: *Father, it's so amazing to think that when I obey You through my persistence and perseverance in hard times, You bless me. Being steadfast sounds so much easier than it really is, but I know I can do all things with Your help.*

Day 12

NEVER BE WORRIED?

*"This is why I tell you to never be worried about
your life, for all that you need will be provided,
such as food, water, clothing—everything your body
needs. Isn't there more to your life than a meal? Isn't
your body more than clothing? Look at all the birds—
do you think they worry about their existence? They
don't plant or reap or store up food, yet your heavenly
Father provides them each with food. Aren't you much
more valuable to your Father than they?"*
MATTHEW 6:25-26 TPT

Have you ever wondered just how to *never be worried*
about your life, like this scripture says? When we're
afraid we're going to lose our home in bankruptcy,
we're supposed to be calm? When we just discovered
those images on our husband's computer for the hun-
dredth time and feel hopeless, we shouldn't be concerned? When the doctor's report came back showing
our greatest fear, worry shouldn't enter the picture?
When we can't find work or are once again a victim of
company layoffs, we are to keep a smile on our face?

Well according to today's scripture, the answer is...*yes.*

But let's look at this honestly because it feels impossible based on the real and immediate situations we face every day. Maybe a more realistic way to process this scripture is to realize we can choose to not *live* in these worries. We can consider our anxiety as nothing more than a valley we pass through on our way to faith.

The reality is that in our human condition, we can't always control our responses to bad news. We can't maintain a sense of calm when we get sucker punched in the gut. When we discover destabilizing information about ourselves or someone we love, we're physically unable to stop our heart from racing in that moment. We hurt. We feel discouragement. We feel helpless. So maybe the idea isn't to bypass our human reactions but to let our faith kick in shortly thereafter.

Friend, God is where you'll find comfort to get through the stressful times you'll inevitably face. He is the One to give peace in the middle of the mess so you can take the next right step. The Lord is deeply invested in your life and promises to go before you, making the crooked path straight as you head toward healing and restoration.

On a very cellular level, you must know this—God's got you. Let this truth sink into the marrow of your bones. Let it become part of your DNA. Because, sweet one, this is how you can stand strong when fear comes barreling your direction without warning. Be quick to remember that God's got you. You can take every bit of stress and fear directly to Him in prayer and He will speak comfort into your weary spirit. He may not calm the storm, but He will calm your heart.

There is a way to live without being overwhelmed with worry and stress. It is possible. And it requires intentional trust in God—the One who has a perfect track record in your life.

ASK YOURSELF THIS. . .

- *Am I a slave to fear and worry right now?*

- *What am I believing that's keeping me stuck?*

- *Do I honestly trust that God will come through and give me His peace?*

- *Where did my beliefs begin, and how do I align them with God's truth?*

PRAYER PROMPTS

Morning: Open up and talk to the Lord about the worries on your heart. Pray something like this: *Father, there are many things that are weighing me down today. I feel overwhelmed with these worries. Sometimes it feels like I am going to drown in my anxiety.*

Afternoon: Ask God to remind you of all the times He came through when you needed it the most. Pray something like this: *Father, when I am stressed out it's hard to remember that You are my deliverer. I forget that You have a perfect track record in my life. And I'm asking You to bring to mind the times where You showed up and made straight the crooked path I was walking.*

Evening: Tell God you need His voice in your life right now. Pray something like this: *Father, would You speak to me and remind me of Your love and power? Would You let Your voice be louder than the fears and anxieties that feel overwhelming? I need You right now!*

Day 13

WORRYING DOES NO GOOD

*Worrying does not do any good; who here can
claim to add even an hour to his life by worrying?*
MATTHEW 6:27 VOICE

What a bold declaration. Jesus is not mincing words here. There are times the Word of God can be a bit confusing or difficult to understand without digging deeper or asking a trusted friend for insight, but this verse is not one of those times. Instead, this is a clear directive. It's a brave statement packed with powerful truth. Maybe the Lord intended it to be plain and simple, so we'd know exactly how He wanted us to live. Because without any misperception and with bold authority, Jesus tells us that our worrying does no good.

Think about it. Being anxious about a teen driver won't make them a better driver. Being scared over finances will never result in more money. Freaking out that your blood test will show something negative won't override the truth. Worrying you may be single forever, that the divorce will always define you, or the ache of being widowed will be constant can't change your circumstances. And obsessing about these never brought peace into your heart.

There will always be something to worry about. Every day, you will have plenty of opportunities to grab on to fears and white knuckle them until you make yourself sick. The reality is that we don't know the future, and that's why we're so scared. We cannot manipulate and control every outcome, even though we give it a college try. And at the root of this worry is a huge uneasiness that no matter what we do, we're going to face horrible outcomes and endings. We think, *What if my best isn't good enough?*

Friend, all of these feelings and emotions are normal. We all experience them from time to time. And while some may worry more than others, the truth is we all worry. We're all left feeling helpless and hopeless to make things happen the way we want them to. But consider that we were never meant to carry our burdens alone. In our humanness, we just cannot.

Chances are you have a friend or two who are always willing to listen to your concerns. Maybe your mom, aunt, or sister is a confidant when stress begins to take its toll in your situation. Is there a coworker you talk to? Maybe a small-group leader? Are there others who love you and are invested in your life? What a gift to have people to support you! But listen up, sweet one. There is no substitute for God—absolutely none.

Even in all their wisdom and kindness and adoration, your earthly support system will never trump the Lord's ability to listen to your anxious heart and heal it. Consider them part of your overall mental health–care team, but never forget that God is number one. He is fully invested in you. He knows the complexity of your emotions. He sees the root of every fear that's taunting you. He completely understands the ins and outs of what's stressing you out. And even more, God knows exactly what you need in that moment.

ASK YOURSELF THIS. . .

- *Do I trust what God says in the Bible?*

- *What am I worrying about the most right now?*

- *Do I believe that I must carry my worry and anxiety alone?*

- *What is the Holy Spirit speaking to me in this moment?*

PRAYER PROMPTS

Morning: Confess the times you've struggled to trust God with your worries. Pray something like this: *Father, I admit there have been circumstances and situations where I chose to not trust You and instead relied on myself. I want to be a woman full of faith instead of doubt. Would You give me the courage to believe You are my Helper even when I cannot see Your face?*

Afternoon: Ask God for reminders that you're not alone to manage stress by yourself. Pray something like this: *Father, would You help me remember that I was not created to manage anxiety alone? You've given me a great earthly support system, but even more You've promised to help me when I need it the most. I'm not built to handle things without You.*

Evening: Tell God what the Holy Spirit has spoken into your heart today. Pray something like this: *Father, I'm so grateful for the gift of the Holy Spirit in my life. He has been ministering to my heart today, telling me things I really needed to hear. I'm humbled and thankful that I am so loved by You!*

Day 14

LEAVE TOMORROW
TO TOMORROW

"Give your entire attention to what God is doing right now, and don't get worked up about what may or may not happen tomorrow. God will help you deal with whatever hard things come up when the time comes."
MATTHEW 6:34 MSG

One of the enemy's greatest schemes is to make us take our eyes off today's stressors and predict what they'll look like tomorrow. Even if you are a cup-half-full kinda girl, he's betting that your predictions will be full of negatives that will create a strong sense of hopelessness. The enemy wants to compound the fear and anxiety you're already feeling because he knows it will bring discouragement. It will make you want to give up and walk away. And chances are it will separate you from God, which is really the enemy's end goal. So if he can get you all stirred up and stressed out and projecting despair about tomorrow, he will consider it a win.

But it doesn't stop there. So often those moments of frustration and fear will make us shut down and suffer *alone.* They have the power to sow seeds of isolation, so we're cut off from our support system. And looking down the road and imagining horrible outcomes and endings makes us feel helpless that things will ever get better. Rather than reaching out for help or going to God in prayer, we become paralyzed. We become ineffective at the tasks at hand, gripped by an over-whelming sense of fear and worry.

Here's the good news, friend. The Lord knows our propensity toward stress and offers a solution—but it's not always an easy one. Reread today's verse. When you start worrying about all the things tomorrow may add to today's troubles, take a step back. Give this day your entire attention. Find God's help for today's challenges. Choose to stay completely focused on what can be accomplished in these twenty-four hours. Tend to the things that need your time and energy between sunrise and sunset today. Be present in the present.

It's hard because it sometimes feels like so much is at stake, and you worry that if you don't plot and plan, things will fall apart. Maybe you believe you're the only one with solutions. Maybe you feel better when you're in control and calling the shots. Maybe you feel responsible for the problems and fixing things will ease your conscience. Whatever the motivation, be brave, sweet one. Find courage to trust God's Word. Rest in knowing that whatever troubles tomorrow may bring, God will be there with you. And just like today, He'll give you exactly what you need to process and resolve and heal and restore.

Keep your eyes on God and your heart full of faith, believing with all your strength that the Lord has gone before you, is standing right next to you, and has your back in all things. Choose to surrender rather than stress.

ASK YOURSELF THIS. . .

- *Am I worrying about tomorrow's stressors?*

- *What do I accomplish by being stressed out about the next day's worries?*

- *How do I respond to stress?*

- *What can I do to stay present in today's struggles and trust tomorrow's to God?*

PRAYER PROMPTS

Morning: Tell God what stressors are pulling your focus into tomorrow. Pray something like this: *Father, I know You tell me to stay focused on today rather than worrying about what tomorrow may bring. Honestly, that is so hard to do right now. There are things that feel too big and too important to put on the shelf. Please increase my faith.*

Afternoon: Ask God to help you respond to stress in healthy ways. Pray something like this: *Father, I'll admit stress makes me do crazy things and feel crazy ways. I know I don't always handle it in the best ways. Would You give me perspective to calm my anxious heart and direct me toward healthy responses so I can stay sane?*

Evening: Thank God that He cares about what you care about and that He is available and ready to meet your needs. Pray something like this: *Father, You are a good God! I'm so grateful that You care enough for me that You promise to never leave me. Thank You for knowing I get stressed and for making a way to help me manage it. I need Your help!*

Day 15

STRESSING OVER
THE DETAILS

*Meanwhile Martha was anxious about all the
hospitality arrangements. Martha (interrupting Jesus):
Lord, why don't You care that my sister is leaving me
to do all the work by myself? Tell her to get over here
and help me. Jesus: Oh Martha, Martha, you are so
anxious and concerned about a million details, but
really, only one thing matters. Mary has chosen that
one thing, and I won't take it away from her.*
LUKE 10:40–42 VOICE

If you remember the story, Jesus and followers had
arrived at the home of Lazarus, Mary, and Martha
in Bethany after breaking their journey. They were
good friends, and these three siblings knew and loved
Him very much. Martha, presumed to be the oldest,
wanted everything to be perfect. She was concerned
about every single detail of the visit, hoping to create a much-needed oasis for Jesus. It was probably
important to her to be known as a good hostess,
ensuring that her guests felt comfortable and cared
for. Chances are she'd started working the minute she
learned they were coming, trying to make her home

feel extra comfy and inviting. Undoubtedly, Martha put much thought into meal prep, hoping to fill the bellies of Jesus and His followers with yummy food. And while her heart in this situation was full of goodness, it was obviously also filling with anxiety.

Mary didn't seem to have a care in the world. While Martha was busy laboring for her guests, her sister sat at the feet of Jesus, listening to His every word. Mary wasn't helping in the kitchen, as was customary during that time. Instead, she spent her time beside Christ. Martha was focused on hospitality while Mary focused on her heart.

Can't we relate to the feelings of this spicy and stressed-out Martha? Think of every big family gathering where we were on the hook for the meal. Think of every holiday hosted in our house and the details involved. Think of celebration planning that fell into our laps. And remember the stress and frustration we felt because we were the ones to do most (if not all) of the prep and cleanup so others could simply enjoy. Rather than enjoy friends and family, we counted the moments until everything was back to some semblance of normal.

What if next time, we chose to balance our Martha tendencies with intentional moments of enjoyment like Mary? What if we decided to sit in the celebration, not worrying if every detail is perfect? What if we delegated duties so we weren't set up for an anxiety-induced breakdown? What if we built in breaks to join everyone else and be part of the gathering?

Deep down, there's a beautiful desire for our labor to make others feel loved and appreciated. We want them to feel valued. And that often manifests as stressing out over the process. But today, decide that going forward you will find balance between juggling the details and joining the celebration.

ASK YOURSELF THIS. . .

- *Am I more of a Martha or a Mary?*

- *Do I end up stressed out instead of enjoying celebrations?*

- *Have I ever asked God to help me with this kind of anxiety?*

- *What needs to change so I can find balance instead of foreboding?*

PRAYER PROMPTS

Morning: Talk to God about your struggles with finding balance between being like Martha and Mary. Pray something like this: *Father, I know You made me on purpose and with intentionality. I understand that who I am is good. But sometimes I struggle to manage the stress that comes from being more like one of these women. Would You give me Your perspective and grace for myself?*

Afternoon: Ask God to help you find joy over stress. Pray something like this: *Father, I don't want to be the kind of woman who is unable to find joy in the juggling. I am designed to take care of those I love, and I really do enjoy celebrating with others. Give me the ability to be joyful rather than full of anxiety over details. Remind me I don't have to be perfect.*

Evening: Ask the Lord to remind you why He made you the way He did. Pray something like this: *Father, I need to be reminded of why You made me the way You did. I know I am not a mistake, but I want to hear that from You. Help me live and thrive in my giftings and find peace in the areas that challenge me the most. Let me see me the way You do.*

Day 16

YOU'RE NOT HERE
TO BE THE SAVIOR

*Pour out all your worries and stress upon him and leave
them there, for he always tenderly cares for you.*
1 PETER 5:7 TPT

Did you notice that today's verse offers a two-step
approach to living a stress-free life? You're being challenged and invited to be completely transparent with
the God who created you and knows you best. And if
taken, you'll be able to find peace in the middle of the
storms you will inevitably face throughout your life.
Let's unpack this today.

Peter tells us to pour out our worries and stresses to
God. He is saying that rather than hold those stressors inside or try to figure everything out by ourselves,
we need to find the courage to tell the Lord all the
ways we are struggling with anxiety. You don't have
to speak the perfect words or find the perfect time.
You can tell Him in the car, lying in bed, or as you
are making dinner. Through tears or in anger, with
grunts and groans or actual words, there is no formula
necessary to make the Lord hear what you need to

say. Honestly, He already knows what is oppressing you. But God also knows the value of sharing what's on your heart.

The truth is that He wants to know how you are doing. He deeply loves and cares for you. And while you may feel like your worries are trivial and the Lord has bigger things to tend to, it's simply not the truth. That theology is incorrect. He wants to know every single fear and frustration assaulting your heart.

So if step one is to bravely share with God your worries and stresses, step two is to release them and leave each of them with the Lord. Can we just be honest for a moment? This will most likely be the hardest thing to do. Why? Because our hearts are tender. We want peace. We care about the outcome. And it feels like a disconnect to not carry the worry of something that really matters to our heart. It feels irresponsible to let it go and not see it all the way to the end. And we're worried that if we hand it over to God, it may get lost somewhere along the way.

Listen up, sweet friend. *You are not God.* Hold on to this truth, because it's a powerful reminder designed to bring freedom and comfort to your heavy heart.

Remember, you're not here to be the savior—not for yourself or anyone else. That role has already been filled by Jesus Himself. And because He understands your human limitations and the ways life stresses you out, the Lord reminds you to lean on Him. He wants to be intimately involved in every part of your worries. He is your safe place to share your heart and your strong tower to protect it. The plan was never for you to carry burdens alone. The plan was always for God to be part of the journey with you.

So go ahead and spill it all. Tell Him what hurts, what scares you, what feels risky, where your insecurities are screaming, and everything in between. Then flex that faith muscle and leave each stress with Him to work out as you walk in freedom.

ASK YOURSELF THIS. . .

- *Why is today's verse hard for me to walk out?*

- *What keeps me from trusting God with my worries and stressors?*

- *Who is God to me?*

- *Do I honestly believe that I am a savior to me or others?*

PRAYER PROMPTS

Morning: Confess the ways stress is beating you up right now. Pray something like this: *Father, I am worried about so many things and can't seem to find peace. I need Your help to manage my anxiety and show me a better way to walk this out.*

Afternoon: Tell God you've struggled to leave your worries with Him. Pray something like this: *Father, it's hard to let go of my concerns once I've shared them with You. So often, I want to pick them back up and try to fix things myself. Help me release control and trust You instead.*

Evening: Ask the Lord to remind you that you are not anyone's savior, not even your own. Pray something like this: *Father, I have such a strong desire to take control and make everything right. I want everyone to be okay. Please remind me that You are God and I am not, and that I desperately need Your help to find balance and peace.*

Day 17

YOU DON'T HAVE TO FIGURE IT ALL OUT

Trust GOD from the bottom of your heart; don't try to figure out everything on your own. Listen for GOD's voice in everything you do, everywhere you go; he's the one who will keep you on track. Don't assume that you know it all. Run to GOD! Run from evil! Your body will glow with health, your very bones will vibrate with life!
PROVERBS 3:5-8 MSG

So much of our stress comes from trying to figure everything out on our own. We tend to take on the whole enchilada rather than delegate small-bite tasks to others. We don't ask for help because our insecurities tell us it's a sign of weakness if we do. Instead of being honest that we're overwhelmed by the situation or unsure of the next right step, we continue to carry the burden silently. Sometimes it's just easier to assume we will figure everything out or at least look like we will. And at the end of the day, we're a hot mess. We're stressed out, frazzled, and barking at those we love.

The missing piece in this scenario is that we aren't trusting God. If we did, our heart wouldn't be troubled and we'd have a sense of peace knowing God is in control. We wouldn't be bogged down with anxiety, sick to our stomachs with concern. If we will choose to humble ourselves and surrender our cares to Him, He promises to keep us on the right track. The Lord goes before you to straighten every crooked path.

Think about your own life for a moment. Where are you trying to figure everything out yourself? You may be a bright and confident multitasker, but we all need help from time to time. You will most certainly need His help to navigate the ups and downs of marriage. You'll need God's perspective so you don't waste time majoring on the minors in life. You will absolutely need His wisdom as you parent kids and His keen discernment as you face other relational challenges. Friend, you will need God's strength to take another step when you're exhausted and His courage to take a stand when necessary. The Lord never intended for you to be alone to try to figure out the struggles and challenges you'll face. In your humanness, you are ill-equipped. That's why He reminds you to ask for His help and listen to His leading.

Even more, there's a promise attached to that reminder. Today's verse says that when we run to God instead of allowing the enemy to stir us up with anxiety, it will positively affect our health. Just like doctors warn us about how stress can hurt our health, God tells us that surrendering our worries to Him improves it! Gone will be the sleepless nights and aching bones. Gone will be the proverbial pit in your stomach. Gone will be the fear and worry that doom is right around the corner.

You don't have to know it all. . .because God does.

ASK YOURSELF THIS. . .

- *What am I trying to figure out on my own that's stressing me out?*

- *What keeps me from asking for help?*

- *Do I trust that God is able and willing to intervene on my behalf?*

- *What do I stand to gain if I invite God into my worries?*

PRAYER PROMPTS

Morning: Confess that you often rely on your own strength and wisdom. Pray something like this: *Father, the truth is that I trust myself more than I trust You sometimes. It may not be a conscious choice; it's just kind of ingrained in my DNA from years of self-reliance. Would You break that in me so I can rest knowing I don't have to figure everything out on my own?*

Afternoon: Share with God what's stressing you out. Pray something like this: *Father, I am so stirred up these days and frustrated that I can't seem to find peace. I am worried about so much, and it feels like a heavy weight on my shoulders that I cannot shake loose.*

Evening: Invite Him into your fears and frustrations, asking for His help. Pray something like this: *Father, I need You. I've tried to handle things on my own, but I'm drowning. Would You please step into the middle of my mess to bring healing and hope? Would You give me direction? I cannot do this without You!*

Day 18

THE STRESS OF
AN UNFAIR LIFE

*"What did I do to deserve this? Did I ever hit
anyone who was calling for help? Haven't I wept for
those who live a hard life, been heartsick over the
lot of the poor? But where did it get me? I expected
good but evil showed up. I looked for light but darkness
fell. My stomach's in a constant churning, never settles
down. Each day confronts me with more suffering. I
walk under a black cloud. The sun is gone. I stand in
the congregation and protest. I howl with the jackals,
I hoot with the owls. I'm black-and-blue all over,
burning up with fever. My fiddle plays nothing
but the blues; my mouth harp wails laments."*
JOB 30:24–31 MSG

Have you ever had a week like this? Can you remember a time when it seemed life blindsided you? You
stood there with arms spread apart thinking, *What just
happened?* There's no doubt we've all faced moments
of shock, trying to make sense of it all.

Maybe a friend betrayed your shameful secret or
your child turned their back on you. Maybe someone
else got the promotion you were promised. Maybe

you didn't get an invitation to the big event or were stuck with the bill. Maybe you were falsely accused. Maybe your spouse or boyfriend changed their mind and left the relationship without explanation. Maybe your identity was stolen or a credit card account was hacked. The reality is that life has a way of not playing fair, and it leaves us scared, angry, worried, and stressed out.

The book of Job gives us an example of this frustrating truth. At Satan's request and God's approval, Job had everything that mattered most stripped away—his animals, his servants, his children, and his own health. In today's verse, Job is crying out to the Lord. He is walking out his emotions, trying to make sense of the situation because he knew he had lived a righteous life. To him, it made no logical sense why these tragedies happened.

What about you, friend? Are you struggling with what's happening in your life right now? Does it all seem unfair? Have you tried to live righteously and are frustrated that hardship continues to come your way?

Just like Job, this is a moment of truth in your walk of faith. This is where you choose to believe God is good and in control, or this is where you choose to live stressed out and angry. This is where you trust that God is allowing this hardship for a good reason, or you decide God has turned His back on you. This is where your faith muscle builds or weakens.

If you read to the end of the book of Job, you'll see the Lord's graciousness in restoring what Job had lost. This was His plan all along. And that's a gold nugget for you to take away. Knowing that life is unfair, trust that God sees your stress. Have faith that He knows what worries you. Talk to Him about it. Open up and share your heart. And then choose to believe God has a plan to restore and heal every bit of it.

ASK YOURSELF THIS. . .

- *Where has life blindsided me lately?*

- *Do I believe that being a Christian means I am protected from stress and hardship?*

- *Am I angry at the Lord for allowing difficulties in my life?*

- *What encourages me from the book of Job and helps to bring perspective and hope?*

PRAYER PROMPTS

Morning: Tell God your misconceptions of being protected by Him because of your faith. Pray something like this: *Father, I confess I've been frustrated that You've not saved me from hard times. Somewhere along the way, I started to believe that being a Christian meant I wouldn't suffer, but I know that's not the truth. Instead, I know You will be with me through the stressful moments life brings. And I am so grateful for that.*

Afternoon: Ask God for perspective when life blindsides you. Pray something like this: *Father, help me be quick to cry out to You when stress and worry take over. Remind me that You are with me, that You are in control, and that You will guide me through it. Build my confidence in Your goodness.*

Evening: Tell God the ways the book of Job encourages you. Pray something like this: *Father, I'm so glad You included the book of Job in the Bible. What a powerful reminder to trust You and allow hardships to build my faith muscle. There is so much I appreciate about his story!*

Day 19

STRESS IN THE LACK
AND ABUNDANCE

---

*I know what it means to lack, and I know what it means
to experience overwhelming abundance. For I'm trained
in the secret of overcoming all things, whether in fullness
or in hunger. And I find that the strength of Christ's
explosive power infuses me to conquer every difficulty.*
PHILIPPIANS 4:12-13 TPT

Stress comes from so many places, doesn't it? Sometimes we feel it in the lack. We lack the financial
resources to meet our monthly obligations. We lack
the patience to answer the four million questions our
small children ask us each day. We lack the forgiveness
needed to reconcile a broken relationship. We lack the
necessary skills to take our career to the next level.
We lack wisdom and discernment to make the best
decisions. We lack motivation to tackle our daunting
to-do list. We lack the available hours to volunteer.
We lack the selflessness to give sacrificially. We lack
the courage to step out of our comfort zone. We lack
the confidence to put ourselves out there *again*.

Other times, we feel anxiety in the abundance. It seems there just aren't enough hours in the day to get everything done. Between running endless errands, carpooling the kids around, figuring out meals for the family, meeting work deadlines, making time for friends, and scheduling a workout, we're completely frazzled by the end of the day. Sometimes, there's just more to do than we can manage, and it stresses us out as we try to be everything to everyone.

Regardless of whether the tension is in the lack or in the abundance, if often manifests the same way. It leaves us cranky and angry at those we love. We're easily frustrated and walk around with a wrinkled brow, barking at friends and family. Rather than offer our help, we feel put-upon by others. Rather than ask for help, we fall into victim mode. And we end up resenting that we have to meet the needs of the ones we really care about, complaining with each task.

What if you changed your perspective? What if instead of giving in to the stress that naturally comes from lack and abundance, you realized your need for the Lord? We get into all kinds of trouble when we decide we're alone in our worry and anxiety. God never intended for you to figure everything out by yourself. And the truth is that life is often way too big for us to navigate without His help. When the lack or abundance threatens your sense of peace, let that be a red flag to take those feelings of stress to God. Paul tells us in today's scripture that doing so will infuse you with His power to conquer every difficulty.

That means you do not have to live stressed out. In every single moment of worry and fear, you can ask for the Lord to give you exactly what you need to manage your overwhelming emotions. You can maintain a peaceful heart even when life is chaotic.

ASK YOURSELF THIS. . .

- *Where am I feeling stress in the lack?*

- *Where am I feeling stress in the abundance?*

- *Do I tend to try to handle my stress on my own, or do I take it to God?*

- *How would stress be more manageable if I asked God for help?*

PRAYER PROMPTS

Morning: Talk to God about your stress in lack and in abundance. Pray something like this: *Father, life is beating me up right now. I'm battling stress in so many areas of my life, and it feels like I'm out of control. If it's not one thing it's another, and I'm losing the peace I so desperately need to live with joy. I cannot continue with these bearing down on me.*

Afternoon: Ask God to intervene and help you navigate those messy situations. Pray something like this: *Father, I simply cannot do this without Your help. Stress is threatening to pull me under, and I am asking for You to intervene. Would You give me a divine perspective so I can see the reality of each stressful situation, and give me peace knowing You are with me no matter what?*

Evening: Confess your tendency to try to handle everything on your own, and thank Him for caring about every detail of your life. Pray something like this: *Father, I confess that I often think I can manage everything without Your intervention. You made me a capable woman, but too often I rely on myself rather than reach out and ask for help. I overestimate my ability. Thank You for caring about me so much that You're willing to help me when I ask. I'm grateful that You truly care about every detail in my life.*

Day 20

FAITH-BUILDING MOMENTS AND FRONT-ROW SEAT SESSIONS

The Lord will fight for you, and you shall
hold your peace and remain at rest.
EXODUS 14:14 AMPC

There are times the Lord requires that you be courageous and stand up for what's right. He wants you to boldly speak up for truth and fearlessly speak out against evil, joining Him in the battle at hand. So often when life is chaotic and tornadic, God asks that you trust Him regardless of what you are seeing in the natural. You're to engage even if it's scary or stress-inducing. It's a call to have epic trust as you take the next step in faith with the Lord.

But there are other times when God's plan is that He alone will battle on your behalf. He isn't recruiting you to fight the anxiety-ridden situation with the Lord's army. Instead, He is requiring you to hold your peace and remain at rest. He's tucking you away while He handles things. Why would He ask this of you in certain circumstances? If scripture says *we can do all things through Christ who strengthens us*, then why wouldn't God want us to be part of the remedy?

Why would He ask us to step aside so He can fix a seemingly irreparable marriage or restore health when doctors have offered little hope? Why would He keep us on the sidelines as He brings home a prodigal child who has wandered far from the way they were raised? Why would God ask us to sit as He reestablishes a relationship that ended in epic betrayal? Why would He require us to not actively defend ourselves as He repairs our reputation that's been trashed by lies? Why would God want us to do nothing in those stressful situations when we feel compelled to handle them on our own?

Consider that those times might be faith-building moments. It may be that God is sidelining you so you'll be able to see His hand at work. It could be His strategy for you to have a front-row seat as you watch Him bring restoration to something broken. These moments may offer you a chance to see His divine intervention because there will be no other explanation. And as you watch the Lord fight for you instead of having to manage things yourself, it will ensure that He will get every bit of the credit. It's not that God needs it; it's that you need to know you're worth fighting for. You need to believe that God sees you in the middle of your stressful mess. And you need to know you're not alone, left to navigate anxiety and worry all by yourself.

Ask God to make clear the times you are to actively engage in the battle with Him, and to make even clearer the times you are to hold on to the peace of Jesus as you watch Him fight on your behalf. There are times for both, and you'll need His wisdom and discernment to know the difference. And when the Lord is telling you to rest as He battles, take it in. Have keen ears and eyes to watch for those faith-building moments and front-row seat sessions.

ASK YOURSELF THIS. . .

- *What is causing me to stress out right now?*

- *Am I supposed to be actively engaged or remaining at rest?*

- *What keeps me from trusting that God will work everything out for me?*

- *Do I see any faith-building moments in my life? If so, how do I need to respond?*

PRAYER PROMPTS

Morning: Confess that you sometimes struggle to trust God will work everything out for you. Pray something like this: *Father, I'll be honest and admit there are times I don't trust You. It's not that I don't believe You're capable. It's that I am not confident that You will take the time. Sometimes I feel my stressors are small in comparison to other things happening in the world that need Your attention. Help me believe that I am worth Your time and effort.*

Afternoon: Ask God to show you the battles you need to fight and the times you need to let Him fight for you. Pray something like this: *Father, please give me the wisdom and discernment to know my place in the battles I'm facing. Too often, I struggle to know if I'm supposed to engage or rest. I need Your help to know what You are requiring of me. I am listening!*

Evening: Thank the Lord for His willingness to be your protector. Pray something like this: *Father, it means so much to know You think I am worth Your time and effort. It grows my confidence and helps to root my self-worth in the right places. The fact that You'd fight for me fills my heart with deep gratitude. In a world where I often feel worthless, thank You for showing me I am not!*

Day 21

THE DOMINO EFFECT
OF AWESOMENESS

Don't run from tests and hardships, brothers and sisters.
As difficult as they are, you will ultimately find joy in
them; if you embrace them, your faith will blossom under
pressure and teach you true patience as you endure.
And true patience brought on by endurance will equip
you to complete the long journey and cross the finish
line—mature, complete, and wanting nothing.
JAMES 1:2-4 VOICE

This is one of those passages that can cause frustration, especially when we're smack-dab in the middle of a hard time. If we're honest, few would agree the stress we are feeling because of a difficult season is seen as a passageway to joy. Most couldn't care less that the worry they're experiencing will ultimately teach patience if handled correctly. The reality is that life is hard, and we are left exhausted by the bumps and bruises along the way. The last thing we want when we're struggling is a Pollyanna response to our anxiety.

But if we can absorb what James is telling us—really embrace this life-changing truth—it will refocus our current perspective and give us hope as we walk through stressful times. It will help us look at seasons of struggle in a different light. Thinking there is some kind of redemption for the tests and hardships we face gives us strength to stand strong through the storms rather than run from them. With God's help, you can endure anything.

Let's not miss the domino effect of awesomeness that comes with choosing to face the stressors that come barreling our way. Friend, every step you take toward God is rewarded by Him. And today's scripture reveals a powerful result should you choose to embrace the less-than-lovely parts of life.

The truth is that the Lord wastes nothing, especially the opportunity to bring good from a spine-weakening situation. Your choice to stay engaged and trust God when life gets hard deepens your faith. And your belief that He is in control and always has your best in mind grows your patience as you wait for Him to show up. And these things work together to equip you to handle whatever comes your way. This mindset calms your anxious heart so you can finish your race with passion and purpose. Sweet one, let this be how you live your life.

Do not be afraid of messiness. Don't hide under your covers when things get hard. Don't find ways to numb yourself in hopes that you don't feel pain.

Do not avoid people or situations that feel difficult to navigate unless God specifically instructs to do so. Don't be a woman who gives up when the going gets tough. Don't allow stress to pull you underwater. Do not let worry and fear render you ineffective. Instead, be a heavyweight in the faith. Know without a doubt that the Lord is in this with you, 100 percent. Trust that the only reason God allows hardships to collide with your life is because He plans to use them for your benefit and His glory. And remember that you are one tough cookie when your main ingredient is faith in God.

ASK YOURSELF THIS. . .

- *What part of this devotional is the hardest for me to embrace?*

- *Do I face my struggles or run from them?*

- *Have I seen God bring good from hardship in the past, either in my life or in someone else's?*

- *What changes am I committed to make today so I can finish my race with passion and purpose?*

PRAYER PROMPTS

Morning: Talk to God about the ways you've been handling hardships. Pray something like this: *Father, after reading today's devotional I'm convinced I need to shift my perspective so I can better handle what is stressing me out. Somewhere along the way, I forgot that faith is the key to living well. I forgot that You are a good God, there to help and guide me. And that hardships are great ways to grow my faith in You.*

Afternoon: Unpack your thoughts about the domino effect of awesomeness. Pray something like this: *Father, it makes a difference for me to know that my stick-to-it mentality comes with benefits. Only You could set up such a reward system. Thank You for using everything for my benefit and Your glory.*

Evening: Tell God your response to today's verse and how it will inform the kind of woman you want to be. Pray something like this: *Father, I'm so encouraged and challenged at the same time. I want to be strong in my faith not only for myself but because I want to influence others to do the same. I want to run this race well and grow my faith every day!*

Day 22

CHOOSING THE ALMIGHTY OVER ANXIETY

For God did not give us a spirit of timidity or cowardice or fear, but [He has given us a spirit] of power and of love and of sound judgment and personal discipline [abilities that result in a calm, well-balanced mind and self-control].
2 Timothy 1:7 amp

Whenever you're battling feelings of being overwhelmed, let it be a big, waving red flag of warning. Let it be like sandpaper on your skin. Let it become so uncomfortable that you must shake it as soon as possible. Why? Because when you are feeling insecure and intimidated by someone or something, when you are stressed and scared to move forward, it's vital to remember those are not God-inspired feelings. You have to know in an instant that something ungodly is coming against you and be quick to rebuke it. Reread today's verse and be reminded that those feelings are absolutely not from Him.

The truth is that our human response often works against us. When we're caught off guard by something that stirs up chaos in our spirit, we usually react with a mix of fear and anxiety. It just spills out without warning as we begin to imagine horrible outcomes and endings, leaving us unsettled. But let's be real here. We can't always help that initial set of emotions. We can, however, choose where to go from there.

So when you're worried about the fight you had this morning with your husband. . .when you're stressed about the mounting bills you can't pay. . .when you're concerned about the meeting your boss just scheduled with you in the middle of company layoffs. . .when you're scared about the choices your child is making. . . when the doctor's diagnosis shakes your foundation . . .don't waste time before you give those insecurities to God. Ask Him to activate your faith response right then and there with the beautiful gifts He created in you. Ask for an immediate reminder that because of Jesus, you have direct access to His power, love, sound judgment, and personal discipline. Choose the Almighty over anxiety.

Here's the best part. When you step boldly into your faith and trust the Lord instead of sinking from the stress, something beautiful happens. Almost miraculously, your anxiety will be replaced by a sense of calm. The doom-and-gloom thoughts that threaten to pull you under will become balanced. And you will have the unexplainable ability to control your emotions rather than allowing them to control you like usual. Peace will return, regardless of the chaos surrounding you.

Friend, stress and worry may always be your first responses when life beats you up, but you don't have to live there. God, in His loving-kindness, made a way for you to get out of that pit of despair, and it requires you to believe you are who God says you are and that He will do what He says He will do. So choose to be the kind of woman who is quick to choose the Almighty over anxiety. And never doubt that God will always come through for you, no matter what.

ASK YOURSELF THIS. . .

- *Do I partner with stress and accept it as part of life?*

- *What aha moment(s) did I get from today's devotional or scripture?*

- *Where am I stirred up right now, and what will I do about it?*

- *How would my life be different if I chose the Almighty over anxiety?*

PRAYER PROMPTS

Morning: Talk to God about the relationship you've had with stress. Pray something like this: *Father, I confess that I have been partnering with stress, and I'm realizing how much it's been hurting me. I live with anxiety and insecurity all the time, and I don't want that anymore. I'm sorry I've forgotten that I can have victory over these things. That's going to change.*

Afternoon: Share with God the things heavy on your heart today and how you're going to respond to them differently. Pray something like this: *Father, I feel overwhelmed with some things in my life. I'm trying to handle them on my own, and it's left me feeling scared and hopeless. Help me remember those feelings aren't from You. Give me the courage to ask for help as I stand in the truth of the strength You created me to access.*

Evening: Tell God how grateful you are that He is always there for you. Pray something like this: *Father, how could I ever do life without You? You really do think of everything, right down to making sure I can steady myself in healthy ways during hard times. Thank You for always being there for me.*

Day 23

THE HOPE WE HAVE IN TROUBLE AND SORROW

"And everything I've taught you is so that the peace which is in me will be in you and will give you great confidence as you rest in me. For in this unbelieving world you will experience trouble and sorrows, but you must be courageous, for I have conquered the world!"
JOHN 16:33 TPT

The Bible is our handbook for living. In its God-inspired pages, we can always find hope and healing. It inspires and encourages us by sharing examples of God's faithfulness. It proves His trustworthiness, patience, and love. The Word helps us understand what we may face in life, giving us a heads-up to what lies ahead. It challenges us to be different and look at situations from an eternal perspective. And it also reminds us of the ways God responds to our needs when we experience hard seasons. Never underestimate the power of His Word and its relevance in your life today.

That's why when you read today's verse from John, you can find peace. It will offer you confidence to know that God is in control and you're not left alone. It will provide the opportunity to rest as you de-escalate from the stress and worry of troubling circumstances.

Sometimes we think that being a Jesus girl means we won't have hard times. We see our *yes* to Jesus as a guarantee of sorts, protecting us from heartache. We decide our belief in Christ promises we will get to bypass anxiety-induced situations. But there is no scripture in the Bible that supports that kind of theology. Instead, we're told trouble and sorrow are inevitable.

Even with our best effort, some marriages will end in divorce. There will be children who will walk away from the faith and instead follow paths that will crush us. Finances will face instability and maybe even fall short. Without warning, our health may fail. Friend-ships may blow up in our face. No doubt, life is hard and full of stressful moments. But because of Jesus, it doesn't end with hopelessness. The Lord is challeng-ing you to be courageous when it feels like things are falling apart. Rather than hide under your covers with a bowl of ice cream, He is encouraging you to grab hold of the bigger picture.

The last part of the verse above is packed with some solid truth. When Jesus says He has conquered the world, it means He has taken the power away from the world to defeat you through the hardships you face.

He disabled their ability on your behalf. So instead of being full of fear and worry, you can rest knowing you can't be beat. You can find comfort remembering the Lord is handling it.

Yes, in this life you will face hard and horrible things. You'll be discouraged and feel overwhelmed. People and situations will beat you down emotionally. There may even be times you want to give up and walk away. But when those times hit, cry out to God to remind you where He is in your mess. Ask Him for help to navigate through the tumultuous waters. And choose to believe that because of Him, you are a capable, strong, powerful woman who can withstand the storm.

ASK YOURSELF THIS. . .

- *Do I believe the Bible in full? Why or why not?*

- *Am I honestly surprised when bad things happen to me, or do I know troubles are just part of life?*

- *How has God assured my victory over things that cause me worry and stress?*

- *What encourages me the most about today's devotional?*

PRAYER PROMPTS

Morning: Confess your struggle with unbelief. Pray something like this: *Father, I admit I sometimes struggle to believe the Bible in its entirety. I forget what it says, especially about how we will face hard times. There are situations where my theology is way off. I'm committed to digging into the Word daily and believing what I read as nonnegotiable truth.*

Afternoon: Tell God where you need His confidence in your life. Pray something like this: *Father, it's so hard to feel strong when I am being beat down. Your Word says You have overcome the world, but sometimes I don't see that. I am weary and stressed out, and I need a big dose of Your confidence to feel secure that things will get better.*

Evening: Thank the Lord for providing rest and hope in the middle of anxiety. Pray something like this: *Father, what a relief to know that even when life feels overwhelming, I can actually live in peace through You. Too often I feel stirred up with stress and strife, and my mind won't stop racing with doom-and-gloom thoughts. Help me rest in You.*

Day 24

YOU'RE NOT ALONE

*So since we stand surrounded by all those who
have gone before, an enormous cloud of witnesses,
let us drop every extra weight, every sin that clings
to us and slackens our pace, and let us run with
endurance the long race set before us. Now stay focused
on Jesus, who designed and perfected our faith. He
endured the cross and ignored the shame of that death
because He focused on the joy that was set before Him;
and now He is seated beside God on the throne, a place
of honor. Consider the life of the One who endured
such personal attacks and hostility from sinners so
that you will not grow weary or lose heart.*
HEBREWS 12:1–3 VOICE

Let's be honest enough to admit that it's not hard to
lose heart when the going gets tough. When we are
in the midst of a mess and trying to figure everything
out, growing weary doesn't take much effort. Life
rarely goes the way we planned, and anxiety can often
tempt us to give up. Sometimes it feels as if we are
carrying the weight of the world on our shoulders, and
we toy with the idea of walking away and starting over.

Take a moment to think of all the things you may be trying to navigate right now that require your endurance. Maybe you're fighting for a child who is battling an addiction and the road has been long and hard. Maybe it's a parent whose health is failing and all the decisions that must be made are overwhelming, especially with the emotions that come with it. Maybe you're engaging in some immoral behavior that's leading you away from what you know is right, and it's hard to fight your way back. Maybe you are struggling with being single, stressed out that your dream of a marriage and a family is slipping away.

It's in these kinds of times we feel so alone. We feel incapable and ill-equipped to handle the worries and insecurities all by ourselves. But when those feelings come, today's verse is the perfect reminder of something very powerful. It confirms that we are not alone, and it encourages us to remember we're not left to walk through tough times without support. Instead, it says we are surrounded by those who have gone before us, and they are cheering us on! They've made the hard journey of faith and finished it well, and now it's our turn to do the same.

Even more, we will find the strength we need to endure by keeping our eyes focused on Jesus rather than the messy, crunchy situations we're in. He too suffered greatly. Jesus braved personal attacks and hostilities of every kind, eventually dying on the cross for speaking truth to the lost. So no, friend. . .you are not alone. Your Savior has gone before you, and many others have too.

Take heart and hold on to this revelation. Be strong and don't allow stress and strife to take you out. God will give you everything you need to run your race with endurance and to overcome anything and everything that threatens your victory. And you'll even have your own cheering section as you do.

ASK YOURSELF THIS. . .

- *How am I doing right now?*

- *What am I facing that makes me feel alone or abandoned?*

- *Have I ever considered that I have a heavenly cheering section of those who have gone before me?*

- *How does that encourage me? What is my response?*

PRAYER PROMPTS

Morning: Share with the Lord the stressors that feel too overwhelming right now. Pray something like this: *Father, I'm worried about several things right now. I am stirred up, and I don't feel like I am handling frustrating areas of my life well. I need Your strength to stay present in my circumstances. Would You help me?*

Afternoon: Talk about your feelings of being alone. Pray something like this: *Father, I feel responsible for fixing the broken things in my life. And I feel it's up to me to find the strength and courage to do it. Your Word says You are always with me, even when it doesn't feel that way. Would You let me feel Your presence?*

Evening: Thank God for a cheering section. Pray something like this: *Father, I love knowing there are those who have already run their race with endurance cheering me on! It brings a smile to my face thinking that I am surrounded by the faithful. Thank You for making that a reality.*

Day 25

SURE AND FEARLESS

God is our shelter and our strength. When troubles seem near, God is nearer, and He's ready to help. So why run and hide? No fear, no pacing, no biting fingernails. When the earth spins out of control, we are sure and fearless. When mountains crumble and the waters run wild, we are sure and fearless. Even in heavy winds and huge waves, or as mountains shake, we are sure and fearless.
PSALM 46:1-3 VOICE

Have you ever considered that when trouble invades your personal space and makes you uncomfortable, the Lord squeezes in even closer? Let's think about that for a moment because it's a profound concept that brings hope to a weary heart.

The psalmist is reminding us that in those times when life feels unbearable, you should press into God. When the bad news comes, He is right there waiting to help. When your to-do list looks overwhelming and you feel unable to make it through the day, He's there to give you strength. When you're feeling attacked from all sides as you stand up for the right thing, God will shelter you. When you fear retribution or condemnation for speaking truth, He will give you confidence to stand your ground. When your relationships feel unstable or unpredictable, God will assure you of His faithfulness. And when you don't feel brave enough to face that situation, the Lord will make you courageous. God is always for you.

The truth is that oppression, fear, and insecurity breed stress, and they are nothing new. They make us worry because they are out of our sphere of control. We feel powerless against them because we can't manipulate the outcomes, and we eventually begin predicting horrible and hopeless endings to the situations we're facing. In the end, we can't seem to shake the feeling that we have failed someone or something. This is why today's passage of scripture is important to cling to. It's a powerful reminder as to why we must invite the Lord into our anxious moments and worrisome seasons. Adding God into the equation gives you everything you need to defeat the enemy of stress. His presence is literally able to fire the stress from bossing you around and make it lose its death grip on your day. The Lord is your shelter and strength, and He is always closer than the trouble you're facing.

So, friend, when you feel stress begin to press in on you, let your faith be where the rubber meets the road. Don't waste your time freaking out or hiding from it. Instead, cry out to the Lord immediately. He will help you be confident and brave. You will find strength to refuse to allow those fears to own you or your day.

You will find the courage to command the flood of anxious thoughts to leave. You'll muster the faith to ask the Lord to replenish your peace. You will be sure and fearless.

Remember that while we will all feel the pangs of anxiety from time to time, we also get to choose what to do with them.

ASK YOURSELF THIS. . .

- *Where do I see God when I'm facing hard times? Is He close or far?*

- *Do I honestly believe God wants me to figure things out on my own? Why?*

- *How do I usually handle stress and worry?*

- *What needs to change so I can be sure and fearless in troubled times?*

PRAYER PROMPTS

Morning: Be honest with God about where you see Him as you face troubles. Pray something like this: *Father, I know Your Word says You are closer than my troubles, but sometimes it's hard to believe it. I feel alone, like I have to figure things out by myself. Build my faith to cry out for Your help. Give me courage to ask when I need it. And give me the willingness to accept Your help when it comes. I don't want to do this without You any longer.*

Afternoon: Confess the unhealthy ways you've handled stress in the past. Pray something like this: *Father, I haven't made the best decisions with how I've dealt with my stress. I've actually chosen very unhealthy options, and I am sorry. I haven't believed You enough to be wise in how I've responded to fear, insecurity, and anxiety. I am committed to doing things differently now, and I'm so grateful Your promise to help never expires.*

Evening: Ask God for courage and confidence to trust Him. Pray something like this: *Father, I am going to take You up on Your offer to be my go-to when troubling times hit. Help me be quick to cry out to You rather than allow stress to pull me down. I want to be known as a woman full of faith, and I need the courage and confidence to walk this level of trust out every day.*

Day 26

A MATTER OF PERSPECTIVE

---

*Whatever you do [whatever your task may be],
work from the soul [that is, put in your very best
effort], as [something done] for the Lord and not
for men, knowing [with all certainty] that it is
from the Lord [not from men] that you will receive
the inheritance which is your [greatest] reward.
It is the Lord Christ whom you [actually] serve.*
COLOSSIANS 3:23-24 AMP

Sometimes it's just a matter of perspective. We can find ourselves bent out of shape for missing the reality of the situation. And often, a little tweak in how we look at things can diffuse the stress we are feeling.

A huge source of anxiety is our propensity to worry about what others think of us. In an effort to please them, we agree to do things we can't easily deliver on. We want to impress, so we bite off more than we can chew. And rather than advocate for ourselves and set healthy boundaries about what we can and cannot do, we want to be considered agreeable.

Our jobs and careers can cause some feather ruffling too. We may not like our boss or we disagree with their way of managing, so our stress level grows every time we're tasked with a project. Maybe we think they show favoritism to others and we lose the desire to do our work well. All that frustration transfers to those in authority over us.

Even more, managing the home front can cause loads of anxiety as well. Between meal planning and car pools, homework and housework, and everything in between, our insecurities can spill over and we take it out on those we love the most. We can become resentful of our crowded calendars and packed to-do lists, and others pay the price. Joy is replaced by bitterness, and home feels more like a battleground.

The Lord knows the stress you're facing. He understands how overloaded you feel at times. And He sees your frustration levels growing. God, in all His love and concern for you, created a way to manage it all. His idea? Change how you see these situations. Realize that every bit of work you do—be it at home, in relationships, or on the job—is to glorify God. Your best effort is for the Lord. Any inconvenience of time or energy is an act of surrender to Him. You are choosing to love and honor those Jesus deeply cares for. And your obedience serves as His hands and feet to others.

Somehow, that tweak in perspective changes everything. It makes the work worth it. It softens your heart to understand your actions are a blessing—an extension of Jesus' love and care for others. It helps the stress diminish because you're not trying to impress anyone. It allows you to see anxiety-inducing people and situations as a mission field of sorts. It matters knowing that the Lord sees the sacrifices you're making and the kindness you're showing. And, friend, He will bless it.

ASK YOURSELF THIS. . .

- *Have I ever considered that my work here on earth is for the Lord?*

- *Where would I say I'm the most stressed and frustrated?*

- *What would it take to tweak my perspective?*

- *How would it help?*

PRAYER PROMPTS

Morning: Talk to God about the stress you're feeling over the work you're tasked with. Pray something like this: *Father, sometimes I feel resentment because it seems I have so much to take care of. When I start to feel caught up, then something else is required. I don't want to let people down. I don't want to fail. And I don't want to feel underappreciated. All these things stress me out, and I'm feeling so overwhelmed right now.*

Afternoon: Share with Him your hesitation with this change. Pray something like this: *Father, honestly, this feels so counterintuitive. It's hard to believe that all I have to do is change my perspective and I'll feel better. I need something to shift soon, so I am going to give it a try. I know Your plans for me are good, and I am choosing to activate my faith and trust You.*

Evening: Ask for His help to tweak your perspective. Pray something like this: *Father, would You give me the confidence and courage to realize everything I do here on earth is actually working for You? I want to please You. I want to honor You. I want to bless You. And knowing that my sacrifice of time and effort glorifies You changes everything for me. Please help me walk this out daily so I can live stress-free and love others at the same time.*

Day 27

HIS PROMISE,
GUARANTEED IN WRITING

Yet when holy lovers of God cry out to him with all their hearts, the Lord will hear them and come to rescue them from all their troubles. The Lord is close to all whose hearts are crushed by pain, and he is always ready to restore the repentant one. Even when bad things happen to the good and godly ones, the Lord will save them and not let them be defeated by what they face. God will be your bodyguard to protect you when trouble is near. Not one bone will be broken.
PSALM 34:17–20 TPT

It's easy to let stress get the best of you. There are plenty of situations that have crushed your heart with unmatched pain and left you gasping for breath. Maybe you've faced a messy divorce or the loss of someone dear to you. Maybe you've had to file for bankruptcy or been diagnosed with a chronic disease. Maybe you're struggling with relationships you thought were solid and watching them fall apart. These are the kinds of things that rock our foundation, shake us to the core, and cause anxiety.

God knew these things were coming and made a steadfast promise of help. We were never told following Jesus meant we'd have stress-free lives, but the Lord is clear that He will rescue us when we ask. He reminds us throughout His Word that He is close to the brokenhearted. And God mentions countless times that He will be our protector. What more could we need?

The problem is that too often, we let stress, fear, and worry rule our days. Rather than cry out to the Lord, we give in to those overwhelming feelings. We choose to sit in our mess when we know that God will make good on His promise to help. Sometimes, we even wear it as a badge of honor because playing the victim has benefits. Staying messy becomes our identity. And we decide that it pays to live in a state of insecurity because it's easier than doing the work with God to heal.

If we are committed to being women of faith, then we simply cannot live in defeat, especially when God has guaranteed us in writing His pledge to hear us, rescue us, and protect us. We have no excuse to stay isolated in our anxiety and worry. There is no reason to cower to the weight of it. Yes, the stress we feel is real and there is no doubt we are going to face it. Yes, there will be seasons and situations when things feel overwhelming and out of control. And yes, we will want to hide away and try to handle things on our own. But decide that from today forward, you will let stress drive you to the Lord. Take God up on His offer to help you navigate the tension and trauma. Trust that He will meet every emotional need you have and will lead you into His peace. Sweet one, God is always for you.

ASK YOURSELF THIS. . .

- *Taking inventory, what situations have crushed my heart lately?*

- *Do I have an expectation that God should be shielding me from stress and pain?*

- *In today's verse, what speaks to me the loudest?*

- *What needs to change so I don't live defeated by anxiety, fear, or worry?*

PRAYER PROMPTS

Morning: Open up to God about the heartbreak you're facing. Pray something like this: *Father, my heart is weary. I'm struggling with so much pain and hurt about some things, and I've tried to handle them on my own. I've either pushed them down or let the pain dictate my mood. I'm realizing that I am not meant to go it alone. I now understand that You have a plan to help me. Thank You!*

Afternoon: Confess your unrealistic expectation of thinking you should never experience hard times. Pray something like this: *Father, I am sorry I've believed wrong for so long. Forgive any resentment I have held toward You. You're a good God who loves me well, and I am grateful for the truth of Your protection and care or me.*

Evening: Tell God how you're going to respond to stress differently. Pray something like this: *Father, I heard You loud and clear today, and I am committed to letting stress drive me to You. Even when I want to hide or handle things myself, I'm going to be quick to cry out for Your help. Thank You for making a way and promising to support me when life feels too big.*

Day 28

ONE MORE TIME
KIND OF FAITH

Don't let them defeat me, Lord. You can't let me fall into
their clutches! They keep accusing me of things I've
never done while they plot evil against me. Yet I totally
trust you to rescue me one more time, so that I can see
once again how good you are while I'm still alive! Here's
what I've learned through it all: Don't give up; don't be
impatient; be entwined as one with the Lord. Be brave
and courageous, and never lose hope. Yes, keep on
waiting—for he will never disappoint you!
PSALM 27:12-14 TPT

How many times have you been in a situation that felt
so overwhelming you just wanted to give up? Can you
recall people who were so messy and full of drama that
you lost hope in having a healthy relationship with
them? Chances are you can! Maybe those you trusted
and loved turned their backs, accusing you of things
you never did or said. Maybe you were abandoned in
troubled times, left to handle something without any
support or help. The truth is that people can be fickle
and often so absorbed in their own stress they don't
notice yours. Even with their best intentions, people
are unreliable. But not God.

Every single time you find yourself freaked out and worried, cry out and share your heartbreak with the Lord again. He never grows weary of hearing from you, His beloved. Friend, He is a *one more time* kind of God, and He'll never run out of patience for your moments of anxiety. Why would He? It's the perfect opportunity for God to remind you of His goodness. And while He does the heavy lifting of rescuing you from the oppression you're feeling, you have a critical part to play.

This is a chance to build more faith. And building more faith takes grit because you're choosing to believe in someone you cannot see with your human eyes or hear with your human ears. All you have—and it's enough—is God's Word and your experiences with Him. You're holding on to the hope He will show up *one more time.* But it's a solid hope, because when you look back at God's fingerprints in your life, you'll see a perfect track record of His faithfulness. He has never let you down. He's never left you in your hopelessness. The Lord has never let you sit in your stress for long. He's never let fear beat you. And God has never let insecurities sink you. When you ask for help, His help always arrives.

So decide today that you won't be a quitter when the going gets tough. Rather than be impatient, know God is busy working out the details for your benefit.

And spend enough time in His Word and in prayer so He is the reason you're full of hope and joy. Ask for the courage to hold on and for His peace as you wait for the *one more time*. He will never disappoint you!

ASK YOURSELF THIS. . .

- *Where do I feel defeated?*

- *Do I really believe God will show up one more time? Or do I think I've asked too much or too often?*

- *What is God's track record in my life?*

- *What changes will I make moving forward?*

PRAYER PROMPTS

Morning: Tell God where you're feeling defeated today. Pray something like this: *Father, I'm pretty stressed out right now because I'm overwhelmed with so many things I cannot control or change. It feels like I cannot catch a break, and so often I want to give up and start over. Why does life have to be so hard? I'm desperate for peace, and I cannot find it without You.*

Afternoon: Ask God to show up one more time. Pray something like this: *Father, sometimes I feel like I ask You for the same things over and over again. I worry You'll get tired of hearing it and will want me to figure things out and move on. But Your Word says the complete opposite, and I am choosing to believe it. You know everything my heart is feeling and needing, and I am asking You to show up one more time. I need You.*

Evening: Tell the Lord you see His hand in your life and thank Him for His faithfulness. Pray something like this: *Father, You are so good to me. When I look back, I can see Your love and care in many of the situations I've faced. Thank You for being involved in the details, big and small. You are so good to me, and I'm grateful for Your fingerprints on my life. I love You!*

Day 29

WHAT TO DO WHEN
YOU WANT TO HIDE

---

*He who takes refuge in the shelter of the Most High
will be safe in the shadow of the Almighty. He will say
to the Eternal, "My shelter, my mighty fortress, my God,
I place all my trust in You." For He will rescue you from
the snares set by your enemies who entrap you and
from deadly plagues. Like a bird protecting its young,
God will cover you with His feathers, will protect you
under His great wings; His faithfulness will form a shield
around you, a rock-solid wall to protect you.*
PSALM 91:1-4 VOICE

Wanting to hide is a natural response to tough situations. When we feel stressed out over a broken relationship or anxious about a chronic health condition, tucking away from life feels safer than facing it. Wanting to climb back into bed often feels like the best option when we're overwhelmed. And powering down emotionally as we binge Netflix and eat cookie dough is sometimes the only option we see. We may be strong women full of faith, but we all have a breaking point. Amen?

What a gift we have in God, though. He understands this tendency. . .this raw need we have to hide. And rather than condemn us or tell us we're cowards and weak women, the Lord decides to become our refuge. He fills the need with His goodness. God becomes our shelter from the storms because He knows we'll be looking for some sort of safe place and He wants it to be Him. God will be a mighty fortress of hope and healing—a place where we can rest our weary hearts. We can lay down every burden, every stressor, every anxious thought, every fear, every insecurity, and every concern, knowing our Father will rescue us every time. He is where we hide when life gets too big.

God never promised us a problem-free life. But He did promise to meet us right in our mess and give us exactly what we needed to work through it. We can shelter in place with God as He guides us to the other side of the issue. So think about it. What is it that you need from Him right now? Is it wisdom and discernment for decisions ahead? Is it strength and endurance to stay engaged in a situation? Is it peace and comfort as you navigate a chaotic circumstance? Do you need joy in your mundane job? Do you need strategy for the stress you're feeling? Maybe you need courage to speak your truth or encouragement that you are good enough. Maybe you need confidence to try again.

Sweet one, when these kinds of situations make you want to run and hide, let them usher you into the Lord's presence. Scripture tells us that God defends His children and will cover and care for you. We're told that His faithfulness will form a shield around you—a rock-solid wall of protection. And while you may not be able to avoid stress and strife, you will always have a safe place with God. When you surrender your worries and fears to Him, He will intervene in magnificent ways.

ASK YOURSELF THIS. . .

- *When life gets hard, do I tend to hide away?*

- *Do I invite the Lord into my stress? Why or why not?*

- *What is it that I need from God right now?*

- *How would sheltering in place with Him help me?*

PRAYER PROMPTS

Morning: Talk to God about the unhealthy ways you've coped with stress in the past. Pray something like this: *Father, I'm realizing I don't always handle my stress well. I'm starting to see unhealthy patterns that lead me into hiding from community. I confess that way too often I turn to the wrong things to manage my fears and insecurities rather than run to You for help and hope. Forgive me and strengthen me as I set out to change my responses to stress.*

Afternoon: Invite Him into your worry and concern. Pray something like this: *Father, I'm learning I cannot handle stress on my own and that I need You to shelter me from its effects. Today, I am asking that You meet me right where I am and give me perspective. I am desperate to feel Your protection from the pain. Would You please defend me and shield me?*

Evening: Tell the Lord what His protection means to you. Pray something like this: *Father, I am so grateful for how You love and care for me. To know that You always have my back gives me courage to keep moving forward even when I am scared and full of anxiety. To realize You will protect me any and every time I need it makes me feel special. You think of everything, and I don't want to do life without You. I love You so much.*

Day 30

THE TRUTH ABOUT STRESS AND STRIFE

We are hedged in (pressed) on every side [troubled and oppressed in every way], but not cramped or crushed; we suffer embarrassments and are perplexed and unable to find a way out, but not driven to despair; we are pursued (persecuted and hard driven), but not deserted [to stand alone]; we are struck down to the ground, but never struck out and destroyed; always carrying about in the body the liability and exposure to the same putting to death that the Lord Jesus suffered, so that the [resurrection] life of Jesus also may be shown forth by and in our bodies.
2 CORINTHIANS 4:8-10 AMPC

Let's remember that feeling pressure is part of the human condition. Let's remember that facing trouble and feeling oppressed from all angles is normal. We will all battle shame and feel stuck in our situation from time to time. We will feel persecution for what we believe in and what we stand for. Feelings of abandonment and rejection will be part of life whether we want them to be or not. So thinking we won't suffer in this life is not only false; it's bad theology. We are broken people living in community with other broken people all trying to figure out life in a broken world. That truth doesn't give us much of a chance to live free from stress and strife. And thinking we can hide our heads in the sand or cross our fingers to somehow escape fear and worry will not make it come to pass.

What if we decided to just recognize these things as normal? What if we chose to have realistic expectations that we'll inevitably face stress and pain? And while we may be caught off guard when hard times hit and hemorrhage fear and anxiety, we can know deep in our DNA that we will not be destroyed.

How can we trust that to be true? Because the Lord has told us He will not allow it. Go back and reread today's passage of scripture. Notice what follows the acknowledgment of stress. Let's personalize it. Read these "I" statements out loud.

No matter what stress and strife come my way. . .I will not be cramped or crushed. I will not be driven to despair. I will not be deserted and left to stand on my own. I will not be destroyed. God is with me to the end.

Hold tight to these truths, mighty warrior. Write them on a note card, take an image with your phone, or tape them to your mirror. This is the perfect bookend to your 30-day challenge to live a less-stressed life because chances are, part of your stress comes from thinking you won't make it through. Today's verses confirm that you most certainly will.

Suffering is a part of life that will never go away until we see Jesus face-to-face. But when you press into the Lord and saturate yourself in the truths found in His Word, you'll find the courage and confidence to thrive, regardless of the stress that surrounds you.

ASK YOURSELF THIS. . .

- *Am I expecting life to be easier than scripture tells me it will be?*

- *How do I honestly feel about suffering?*

- *Do I believe the Lord will protect me? Why or why not?*

- *What is my biggest takeaway from today?*

PRAYER PROMPTS

Morning: Confess your unrealistic expectations. Pray something like this: *Father, I thought life as a Jesus girl would be easier than it is. I think I hoped You would exclude me from any stress and fear. Please forgive me for the times I've been angry at You when something went wrong. I confess that my theology was off base, and I am sorry for any resentment I've carried toward You in my heart. I now understand the truth that You are with me through the hard times!*

Afternoon: Thank the Lord for His protection and promise. Pray something like this: *Father, what a relief to know You will take care of me. For so long, I tried to handle things on my own, and that hasn't always gone so well. I need Your protection as I navigate the ups and downs of life, and I feel so much better knowing that You promise to keep me from crumbling under the weight of stress.*

Evening: Tell God how He has spoken to you through this 30-day challenge. Pray something like this: *Father, thank You for meeting me in the pages of this book. You have ministered to my stressed-out heart in powerful ways. I never realized You had so much to say about anxiety and worry, and it's been eye-opening to read scripture that has spoken directly to my situation. I love You and am so thankful You are willing and able to help me!*

SCRIPTURE INDEX